MACAT

An Analysis of

James March's

Exploration and Exploitation in Organizational Learning

T0349762

Pádraig Belton

ROUTLEDGE

Published by Macat International Ltd
24:13 Coda Centre, 189 Munster Road, London SW6 6AW.

Distributed exclusively by Routledge
2 Park Square, Milton Park, Abingdon, Oxon OX14 4RN
711 Third Avenue, New York, NY 10017, USA

Routledge is an imprint of the Taylor & Francis Group, an informa business

www.macat.com
info@macat.com

Cataloguing in Publication Data
A catalogue record for this book is available from the British Library.
Library of Congress Cataloguing-in-Publication Data is available upon request.
Cover illustration: A. Richard Allen

ISBN 978-1-912303-98-4 (hardback)
ISBN 978-1-912284-69-6 (paperback)
ISBN 978-1-912284-83-2 (e-book)

Notice

CONTENTS

THE MACAT LIBRARY

The Macat Library is a series of unique academic explorations of seminal works in the humanities and social sciences – books and papers that have had a significant and widely recognised impact on their disciplines. It has been created to serve as much more than just a summary of what lies between the covers of a great book. It illuminates and explores the influences on, ideas of, and impact of that book. Our goal is to offer a learning resource that encourages critical thinking and fosters a better, deeper understanding of important ideas.

Each publication is divided into three Sections: Influences, Ideas, and Impact. Each Section has four Modules. These explore every important facet of the work, and the responses to it.

This Section-Module structure makes a Macat Library book easy to use, but it has another important feature. Because each Macat book is written to the same format, it is possible (and encouraged!) to cross-reference multiple Macat books along the same lines of inquiry or research. This allows the reader to open up interesting interdisciplinary pathways.

To further aid your reading, lists of glossary terms and people mentioned are included at the end of this book (these are indicated by an asterisk [*] throughout) – as well as a list of works cited.

Macat has worked with the University of Cambridge to identify the elements of critical thinking and understand the ways in which six different skills combine to enable effective thinking.
Three allow us to fully understand a problem; three more give us the tools to solve it. Together, these six skills make up the **PACIER** model of critical thinking. They are:

ANALYSIS – understanding how an argument is built
EVALUATION – exploring the strengths and weaknesses of an argument
INTERPRETATION – understanding issues of meaning

CREATIVE THINKING – coming up with new ideas and fresh connections
PROBLEM-SOLVING – producing strong solutions
REASONING – creating strong arguments

To find out more, visit **WWW.MACAT.COM.**

CRITICAL THINKING AND "EXPLORATION AND EXPLOITATION IN ORGANIZATIONAL LEARNING"

Primary critical thinking skill: EVALUATION
Secondary critical thinking skill: REASONING

James March is an outstanding example of an evaluative thinker at work. In "Exploration and Exploitation in Organizational Learning," he not only delves in great detail into economists' existing arguments about organizations, which portray them as rational, unified actors that act with perfect information, and evaluates why these are wrong; he also adeptly chaperones us through a vast number of arguments, drawn from political science, economics, and sociology, and evaluates them in detail for usefulness in building up an understanding of how organizations process and store information and make decisions.

First marshaling their arguments, March identified areas of weakness, mainly in their behavioralism, which after World War II sought to systematize and quantify the social sciences. March judged these arguments as lacking, reasoning that if such highly simplified models of businesses assume decision-makers always act with complete information, then these models will not advance understanding of how businesses learn.

March reasoned that the internal structure of a business will reveal a great deal about how businesses learn and make strategic decisions. By then looking in scholarly detail at how businesses formed only of fast or slow learners will behave, he evaluated the strengths of both and used those conclusions to reason that a business with a mixture of fast and slow learners will outperform one with a workforce that is homogenous. March argued that fast learners will adapt quickly, but slow learners will preserve useful lessons in the organizational code.

This strong emphasis on evaluating useful contributions from an astonishing variety of social science disciplines, and detailed reasoning about how businesses will learn and make strategic decisions, is a defining feature of March's work.

ABOUT THE AUTHOR OF THE ORIGINAL WORK

Stanford academic **James March** is one of the twentieth century's leading scholars of organizations, contributing greatly to our understanding of how they learn and the ways they make decisions. Aside from "Exploration and Exploitation in Organizational Learning," he is well known for his contributions to the field of organizational studies, his Garbage Can model of decision-making, and his breadth of work for both public and academic audiences, including several books of poetry and two films.

ABOUT THE AUTHOR OF THE ANALYSIS

Pádraig Belton was educated at Yale, Oxford, and the School of Oriental and African Studies. He has received a Fulbright fellowship and the Royal United Services Institute's Trench-Gascoigne Prize for writing in foreign affairs. A journalist, he contributes for the BBC, *Times Literary Supplement, Spectator,* and S&P's financial newswire.

ABOUT MACAT

GREAT WORKS FOR CRITICAL THINKING

Macat is focused on making the ideas of the world's great thinkers accessible and comprehensible to everybody, everywhere, in ways that promote the development of enhanced critical thinking skills.

It works with leading academics from the world's top universities to produce new analyses that focus on the ideas and the impact of the most influential works ever written across a wide variety of academic disciplines. Each of the works that sit at the heart of its growing library is an enduring example of great thinking. But by setting them in context – and looking at the influences that shaped their authors, as well as the responses they provoked – Macat encourages readers to look at these classics and game-changers with fresh eyes. Readers learn to think, engage and challenge their ideas, rather than simply accepting them.

'Macat offers an amazing first-of-its-kind tool for interdisciplinary learning and research. Its focus on works that transformed their disciplines and its rigorous approach, drawing on the world's leading experts and educational institutions, opens up a world-class education to anyone.'

Andreas Schleicher
Director for Education and Skills, Organisation for Economic
Co-operation and Development

'Macat is taking on some of the major challenges in university education … They have drawn together a strong team of active academics who are producing teaching materials that are novel in the breadth of their approach.'

Prof Lord Broers,
former Vice-Chancellor of the University of Cambridge

'The Macat vision is exceptionally exciting. It focuses upon new modes of learning which analyse and explain seminal texts which have profoundly influenced world thinking and so social and economic development. It promotes the kind of critical thinking which is essential for any society and economy.
This is the learning of the future.'

Rt Hon Charles Clarke, former UK Secretary of State for Education

'The Macat analyses provide immediate access to the critical conversation surrounding the books that have shaped their respective discipline, which will make them an invaluable resource to all of those, students and teachers, working in the field.'

Professor William Tronzo, University of California at San Diego

WAYS IN TO THE TEXT

KEY POINTS

- James March did postgraduate study at Yale University and spent most of his teaching career at Stanford University.

- He developed a robust framework to link two approaches an organization can choose to pursue: innovating, or exploiting competitors' innovations and outperforming them.

- March's study helped create a field of modern organizational theory,* and shed light on companies and the ways they learn.

Who Is James March?

Born in 1928 in Cleveland, Ohio, James March grew up there and in Madison, Wisconsin. He studied political science at the University of Wisconsin, interrupting university from 1946 to 1948 to serve in the US army, and then returned to complete his degree. A keen student, he then went to Yale University where he received his master's degree and doctorate in political science, while also attending lectures in a broad number of other social science disciplines, such as sociology, economics, and anthropology.

March then began an academic career, first at the Carnegie Institute of Technology, then at the University of California, Irvine, and finally at Stanford University where he would spend most of his life.

His principal interest, as an academic, was how organizations behave, learn, and make decisions. His work in the field of organizational theory* combined insights from psychology, economics, sociology, and political science. These are the key questions he addresses in "Exploration and Exploitation in Organizational Learning."

These interests in understanding how organizations learn and behave began during March's time at the Carnegie Institute of Technology, where he was influenced by—and formed part of—the Carnegie School.* Along with Carnegie School colleagues like Herbert Simon* and Richard Cyert,* March called into question the received wisdom that businesses understand their environments perfectly, and behave rationally. Instead, the Carnegie School asked how different groups within a company—managers, stockholders, workers—might have different goals, as well as information and priorities.

March, along with Richard Cyert, helped create a behavioral* approach that understands businesses not as unified actors, but as coalitions of these different groups. In turn, those groups argue over the company's goals, about production, market share, inventory, and sales.

March's curiosity about understanding how organizations behave, learn, and make decisions continues to be the strongest theme in his research, including after he moved to Stanford. He created an influential Garbage Can Model* of interpreting how organizations make decisions, which he worked on with Johan Olsen* and Michael Cohen.* This model says it is too simplistic to think organizations start with problems and work towards their solutions. Instead, March and his coauthors said, problems, possible solutions, participants, and opportunities to make choices all are stirred about in an organization, which March and the others likened to a garbage can.

Along with entirely changing the way we look at businesses and other organizations, March has also published eight volumes of poetry, and is responsible for two films.

What Does "Exploration and Exploitation in Organizational Learning" Say?

March's study "Exploration and Exploitation in Organizational Learning" first and foremost provides readers with a strong and valuable framework to compare two very different options that are open to businesses and other organizations that compete with each other.

Organizations have scarce resources, therefore, they must choose whether to innovate, or to copy the innovation of others, and use their resources to make improvements in the areas of efficiency, production, and execution.

That, for March, is the key decision facing every business. They must engage in a trade-off between innovation, which he calls "exploration* of new possibilities," and adapting and refining the innovations of others, calling this "exploitation* of old certainties."[1]

Returns from exploration are also less certain, further away in time, and may benefit different parts of an organization. Basic research, or the search for new ideas or markets, may not pay off for some time, if at all, and when it does, the payoff may go to a different person within the organization rather than the one making the decision.

March said that exploitation is likely to be effective in the short run, but investing in innovation is better over the longer term. Exploitation, he said, is even self-destructive in the long run.

According to March, well-socialized and trained workers have less variability in skill from worker to worker, which makes for a more reliable workforce. Although by having less variability, that same workforce may also find itself less likely to make discoveries that would put that company in front of its peers. March referred to a physicist, Michael Polanyi,* as saying he never would have conceived of his theory, or made great efforts to verify it, if he had been more conversant with major contemporary developments in physics.

Learning and imitation inhibit experimenting, March argues: "reason inhibits foolishness," as he puts it.[2]

Why Does "Exploration and Exploitation in Organizational Learning" Matter?

It is hard to overstate the importance of "Exploration and Exploitation in Organizational Learning," a contribution that tends to be called things like "pioneering."[3] The *Economist* described March as the "guru's guru" for his work on how organizations behave.[4]

A political scientist at the University of Chicago, John Padgett,* wrote in an academic journal that "Jim March is to organization theory what Miles Davis is to jazz... March's influence, unlike that of any of his peers, is not limited to any possible subset of the social science disciplines; it is pervasive."[5]

In fact, Padgett follows this claim up with a chart, showing March is broadly cited across at least eight fields: business studies, sociology, political science, psychology, economics, law, public policy, and education. A search on the Google Scholar search engine, meanwhile, reveals 19,709 scholarly articles altogether that have cited March's study.[6]

It is counterintuitive to think that imitation, and borrowing and refining the discoveries of others, might be an equally valid route to success as pursuing new inventions and discoveries. But March pointed out the validity of both paths, and also the attractions and drawbacks of each. He also drew a more interesting picture of the businesses that make these decisions, telling us they are not unitary actors, but describing them instead as heterogeneous coalitions made up of many employees with different roles, information, and agendas.

Understood and used properly, March's categories of exploration and exploitation, and contrasting innovation with imitation and refinement, will help readers understand the decisions businesses must regularly make in a new, illuminating way.

March also expanded these ideas in a book with Johan Olsen, *Democratic Governance* (1995), and his later work, *The Pursuit of Organizational Intelligence* (1999), with an increasing shift towards looking at how organizations learn.

His powerful framework, combined with the set of questions he posed—pivotal in producing the new academic field of behavioral economics*—has given rise to a broad set of research projects that incorporate psychology, sociology, political science, and economics in exciting ways, and combines them to yield deeper understandings of organizations and how they make decisions.

March received many accolades for "Exploration and Exploitation in Organizational Learning," including an award for excellence in teaching at Stanford in 1995, a Norwegian knighthood the same year, and the Order of the Lion, a Finnish state honor, in 1999. He was elected to the American Philosophical Society in 2001, and the American Political Science Association also gave him its Aaron Wildavsky Enduring Contribution Award in 2004.

A quarter century after its publication, "Exploration and Exploitation in Organizational Learning" remains indispensable reading for anyone interested in understanding how businesses learn and make decisions, in particular, whether to pursue innovation or to copy the innovations of others better.

NOTES

1   James G. March, "Exploration and Exploitation in Organizational Learning," *Organization Science* 2, no. 1 (1991): 71.

2   March, "Exploration and Exploitation in Organizational Learning," 73.

3   A Gupta et al, "The Interplay Between Exploration and Exploitation," *Academy of Management Journal* 49, no. 4 (2006): 693-706.

4   "James March," *The Economist*, July 24, 2009, accessed December 19, 2017, http://www.economist.com/node/14099644.

5   John F. Padgett, "Learning From (and About) March," *Contemporary Sociology* 21, no. 6 (1992): 744.

6   Google Scholar, https://scholar.google.co.uk, accessed December 18, 2017.

SECTION 1
INFLUENCES

MODULE 1
THE AUTHOR AND THE HISTORICAL CONTEXT

KEY POINTS

- "Exploration and Exploitation in Organizational Learning" ushered in a new way of understanding how businesses and other organizations learn and make decisions.

- March's education at Yale exposed him to insights from sociology, anthropology, and economics, and lent his work an interdisciplinary character he retained his entire career.

- "Exploration and Exploitation in Organizational Learning" has deeply influenced how we why businesses sometimes are not unified, may at times not behave rationally, and often have only imperfect knowledge of their surroundings, groups, and societies.

Why Read This Text?

With "Exploration and Exploitation in Organizational Learning," James March's impact on the way we understand how organizations learn and arrive at decisions is profound. One journal article from 2017 calls it, "a good example of a blockbuster paper."[1] March's idea that organizations need to make choices, particularly between new discoveries and gaining efficiencies in things they already know, now is a common one. Although, just because March's key arguments about whether businesses explore or exploit are nearly universally used now across academia and business does not mean they are always used properly. Getting these concepts second hand could mean ending up with understandings that are both inaccurate and incomplete.

This is partly because March's model is rich with paradoxes. For

❝ What is good in the long run is not always good in the short run. ❞

James G. March, "Exploration and Exploitation in Organizational Learning"

instance, even though exploring is better than exploiting over the long term, the reverse is true in the short term. By rigorously training its staff, an organization can become very good at exploiting, but reduce the intellectual diversity that is necessary for exploring. Similarly, organizations that have both "smart" and "slow" learners outperform ones that only have "smart" learners. Slow learners preserve collective wisdom better, whereas smart learners might be quick to respond to fads or to overspecialize.

Reading "Exploration and Exploitation in Organizational Learning" is key to applying correctly its important arguments about the organizations, whether businesses or not-for-profit bodies, that surround us everywhere. These concepts include the ideas that all organizations are capable of learning; that procedures, norms, rules, and forms in an organization together constitute a type of knowledge; and that organizations learn to retain and improve productivity, innovation, and advantage over their competitors.

March's framework helps us to understand that organizations, even if they are less than perfectly rational and have less than complete knowledge of the world around them, still can evolve collective behaviors that are intelligent, adaptive, and creative.

People live surrounded by organizations in all directions, as their employers, clients, and providers on whose goods and services they depend. Understanding how these organizations behave, make decisions, and learn will make us better managers or employees, customers, and citizens, and nudge us toward comprehending our social surroundings just a little better.

Author's Life

James March was born on January 15, 1928, in the American mid-west. His family lived initially in Cleveland, Ohio, although they moved when he was nine to Madison, Wisconsin.[2] In his teenage years, he particularly enjoyed both sports and mathematics; he describes himself as captaining his junior high-school football squad, while taking every mathematics course available.[3]

Briefly considering a military career, he received offers from the US Military Academy and US Naval Academy, but instead accepted a place at the University of Wisconsin, where he chose to study political science. He then interrupted his studies to serve in the US army from 1946 to 1948, including a period of service in Japan. In 1949, he came back to Wisconsin to complete his degree. His earlier interests in mathematics persisted, and he supplemented his political science coursework with classes in public finance and statistics.

Immediately after, he went on to graduate school at Yale University, where he described himself in the preface to his doctorate as "a Wisconsin innocent."[4] He received a master's degree in political science in 1950, and his Ph.D. three years later.

After spending eleven years teaching at the Carnegie Institute of Technology (now Carnegie Melon University), and another six as a professor of psychology and sociology at the University of California, Irvine, he moved in 1970 to Stanford University as a professor, where he remained for the rest of his teaching career.

Unusually for a professor who is well known for his academic work, March has also published eight collections of poetry. He also wrote two films jointly with documentary producer Steven Shecter.* These present lessons in leadership drawn from *War and Peace** and *Don Quixote.**

Author's Background

March's work in "Exploration and Exploitation in Organizational Learning" reflects strong influences both from his time at Yale, and his first decade teaching at the Carnegie Institute of Technology.

The political science faculty at Yale when March arrived was highly torn apart by academic politics. As he commented in the preface to his dissertation, "one large segment of the faculty had recently left in a huff [and] several senior faculty members were hardly talking to each other."[5]

As a result, March spent a great deal of time reading in Yale's main library, and being influenced by people in disciplines outside his department. The interdisciplinary flavor of his time at Yale made him happy to live in many disciplines all at once throughout his academic career.

One of these influences came in economics courses which he took from Charles Lindblom,* who worked on incrementalism* in policy making. Anthropologist George Peter Murdock,* who looked at kinship networks,* was another particular influence on March, as was sociologist Fred Strodtbeck,* who studied values in small groups.

When March completed his doctorate and went on to teach, he was strongly affected by a group of academics, later known as the Carnegie School, who were inventing a new field of behavioral economics.* Many researchers who worked within neoclassical economics,* which dominated departments at the West and East Coast universities (and which was sometimes called "seawater economics"*), tended to look at businesses as unified, rational actors, with perfect knowledge of their environment. As a benefit of using simplified abstractions of businesses like these, they then were able to develop mathematics to make predictions about how they interact with each other in markets.

The Carnegie School took another approach and suggested instead that businesses were not unified, that they did not behave rationally, and they had only imperfect knowledge of their surroundings.

Instead of beginning with highly simplified understandings of organizations, March and his colleagues looked into how scholarship could start by examining how organizations encompass many roles, each having different priorities and information. Since the people who posed these sorts of questions often were in mid-western universities, such as Carnegie and the University of Chicago, they were often referred to as "freshwater" economists* because they were nearer the Great Lakes than the oceans.

These concerns about understanding the messier ways organizations behave in the real world were the ones March continued to explore even after he moved to Stanford, where he spent most of his career.

Beyond these main driving concerns in March's scholarship, he also is a polymath who draws ideas from a broad range of disciplinary perspectives. In his teaching career alone, he taught courses on such an astonishing large range of subjects as friendship, revolutions, rules for killing people, computer simulation, and statistics.[6]

NOTES

1 Johann Peter Murmann, "More Exploration and Less Exploitation," *Management and Organization Review* 13, no. 1 (2017): 5.

2 Faculty curriculum vitae at University of Stanford, <https://sociology.stanford.edu/sites/default/files/jgmvita.pdf>, accessed Dec. 16, 2017.

3 Morgen Witzel and Malcom Warner, *The Oxford handbook of Management Theorists* (Oxford: Oxford Univ. Press, 2014), 409.

4 James G. March, *Autonomy as a Factor in Group Organization: A Study in Politics* (Doctoral dissertation, Yale University, 1953), iii.

5 March, 1953, iii.

6 Timothy Hindle, *Guide to Management Ideas and Gurus*, (Suffolk: Profile Books Ltd, 2008).

MODULE 2
ACADEMIC CONTEXT

KEY POINTS

- The field of organization studies began in the late 1940s, when US academic departments began confidently applying scientific methods (behavioralism) to understanding questions in social sciences.

- March rejected the first generation of behavioralist* work, arguing that research such as economists' theory of the firm was excessively simplified and reductionist.

- He wrote in the non-behavioralist tradition of research.

The Work in Its Context

March wrote in a tradition of organization studies,* which he thought of as beginning in North America immediately after World War II.*[1] The quickly growing US economy in the postwar years attracted heightened attention from university departments, whose faculties were increasingly bolstered by immigrant academics from Europe.

This new discipline of organization studies, which attracted the energies of March along with his frequent coauthors, cognitive scientist Richard Cyert* and economist Herbert Simon,* emerged from more established academic disciplines: from psychologists who were interested in groups, sociologists who were interested in institutions, economists interested in the firm, and political scientists interested in bureaucracies. A common theme uniting them was their attempt to make studying human behavior and institutions more scientific. All social science disciplines now aspired to an ideal of behavioralism* that sought to identify universal truths, through more refined techniques for gathering quantitative* data and conducting

> ❝ Both exploration and exploitation are essential for organizations, but they compete for scarce resources. As a result, organizations make explicit and implicit choices between the two. ❞
>
> James G. March, "Exploration and Exploitation in Organizational Learning"

multivariate analysis* of it.[2] This behavioralist tradition began at the University of Chicago, in works like Charles Merriam's* 1903 book *A History of American Political Theories*. Merriam, serving as chairman of Chicago's political science department from 1911, significantly influenced the way political science developed across the United States in the 1920s and 1930s, borrowing statistical techniques from mathematics and economics, and making ample use of concepts from psychology. By the 1960s and 1970s, conducting research in the behavioralist tradition was becoming mainstream among most university social science departments, while a handful (like British political scientist Sir Bernard Crick*) remained devoted to less mathematical modes of research, and pointed out failings in the now dominant behavioralist approaches.

Against this backdrop, in 1958, the Anglo–American economist Kenneth Boulding* wrote that the new field of organizational studies, in its aim to come up with a behavioralist general theory of organizations, was trying to separate itself from these parent disciplines. At the same time, it was fundamentally dependent on developments in those same older disciplines for a successful take-off.[3]

Two decades later, March's "Exploration and Exploitation in Organizational Learning," and his other works (both on his own and with coauthors) helped organization studies arrive at maturity as a discipline, able to engage other social sciences but also to criticize shortcomings in their approaches. For instance, March points out that economists' highly simplified understandings of organizations led them to ignore both ways they do not behave as unified units, and times they do not act with perfect information of their surroundings.

Since March, other scholars have helped expand further on the themes he identified in his work to explore how organizations learn in such areas as collaboration, joint ventures, innovation, technology adoption, and market orientation.

Overview of the Field

March touches in "Exploration and Exploitation in Organizational Learning" on a number of different research questions about organizations. These include how businesses learn, how they make decisions, and how they are structured. In each of these, he argues with received wisdom created by the first generation of behavioralist scholars in the 1950s and 1960s.

An example is the neoclassical, economic view of businesses that comes from the work of Richard Coase,* a British economist who from 1964 taught at the University of Chicago law school. For Coase, businesses exist to minimize transaction costs.* Transaction costs are costs incurred by the act of buying, instead of reflecting the price of the actual good or service. Searching for goods, gathering information, bargaining, and then making sure another party sticks to the term of the agreement are each examples of transaction costs. For Coase, transaction costs are why people band together in businesses: businesses provide ways of mitigating transaction costs at least for transactions internal to them.

March—both in "Exploration and Exploitation in Organizational Learning" and in the earlier 1963 book *A Behavioral Theory of the Firm* he wrote together with Richard Cyert—argued that the neoclassical approach was built on incorrect assumptions, especially perfect knowledge and that firms maximize* their profits.

The theory of the firm he proposed instead, which he called the behavioral theory of the firm,* looked at businesses as coalitions, with managers, stockholders, and workers possibly having different priorities and information. March's view of businesses-as-coalitions fit in with his view of decision making-as-satisficing: a unified actor with perfect information can attempt to maximize profits, but a coalition with different information and priorities more likely pursues goals that are compromises.

As well as the behavioral theory of the firm that March and his coauthors developed, there were also other responses to the neoclassical understanding of businesses. One is the managerial theory of the firm*: for economists like William Baumol* and Oliver Williamson,* this means examining how shareholders and executives may have different priorities.

Academic Influences

One particularly important influence on March was Austrian-American economist Joseph Schumpeter*, who was likely the first scholar to think through the implications of entrepreneurialism,* which he described in a 1947 article as "the doing of new things or the doing of things that are already being done in a new way."[4]

This innovation and technological change relies chiefly on individuals' creativity, though for Schumpeter, large businesses' resources are needed too, and being an entrepreneur is more than just being an inventor. An entrepreneur is also an innovator, who can displace old structures and replace them with new ones. Capitalism releases disrupting streams of innovation, which Schumpeter memorably calls a "gale of creative destruction": this gale is a "process of industrial mutation" continually changing the economic structure from within."[5]

Herbert Simon was a second postwar academic whose ideas strongly influenced March. While previous economists had assumed firms to be perfectly rational, Simon disputes this in the 1947 book, *Administrative Organization* (the judges called this book "epoch-making" when they awarded Simon the Nobel Prize for Economics in 1978).[6] For Simon, real businesses have only fragmentary knowledge of the consequences that will ensue from each choice they are contemplating. They also cannot choose between all possible alternative actions, but must only concentrate on a few. Simon calls this behavior satisficing: looking for a course of action that is not perfect, but is satisfactory.

While March drew for his ideas on innovation on Schumpeter, and on Simon for his approach that organizations make best-possible (satisficing) decisions, a third influence came from a 1978 book (and earlier 1974 article) by Harvard Business School professor Chris Argyris* and Massachusetts Institute of Technology (MIT) academic Donald Schön,* called *Organizational Learning.*[7]

There are two sorts of learning for Argyris and Schön. One is like a thermostat adjusting the temperature because it is too hot or cold (they call this "single-loop learning"*): this is when an organization can receive information and take corrective action, with an emphasis on techniques and making them more efficient. More thoroughgoing learning happens when an error is detected that, to be corrected, requires modifying an organization's basic policies, norms, or objectives ("double-loop learning"*).

While these two authors use the terms "single-loop" and "double-loop" learning, the concepts are similar to the ones March developed, called exploitation and exploration.

NOTES

1   Mie Augier et al, "The Evolution of a Research Community: Organization Studies in Anglophone North America, 1945-200," *Organization Science* 16, no. 1 (2005): 85-95.

2   James March, "The Study of Organizations and Organizing Since 1945," *Organization Studies* 28, no. 9 (2007): 11-12.

3   Kenneth Boulding, "Evidences for an Administrative Science: A Review of the *Administrative Science Quarterly*, Volumes 1 and 2," *Administrative Science Quarterly* 3, no. 1 (1958): 1-22.

4   Joseph Schumpeter, "The Creative Response in Economic History," *Journal of Economic History* 7 (1947): 149–59.

5   Joseph Schumpeter, *Capitalism, Socialism and Democracy*, (London: Routledge, 1994 [1942]), 82–83.

6   Press Release, Royal Swedish Academy of Sciences, October 16, 1978. (Online at <https://www.nobelprize.org/nobel_prizes/economic-sciences/laureates/1978/press.html>, accessed December 20, 2017).

7   Chris Argyris and Donald Schön, *Organizational Learning: A Theory of Action Perspective* (Reading, Massachusetts: Addison-Wesley, 1978). *Theory in Practice: Increasing Professional Effectiveness*, (San Francisco: Jossey-Bass, 1974).

MODULE 3
THE PROBLEM

KEY POINTS

- For March, deciding whether to explore or exploit is a vexing dilemma for businesses, since what is good in the long run (innovation, normally) is not always so in the short term.

- March rejected the rational choice* tradition, and instead drew on other concepts, among them William Whyte's organization man and Paul David's theories of innovation.

- Contemporary debate about organizations includes divisions over whether approaches should prioritize structure or agency, and debates between top-down and bottom-up perspectives.

Core Question

In "Exploration and Exploitation in Organizational Learning," James March asked exactly how organizations decide whether to develop wholly new technologies and products ("exploration") or just to tinker with and improve upon the innovations of their competitors ("exploitation").

It is a dilemma, said March. On the one hand, he stated, it is clear that exploring new technologies reduces the speed at which a business betters its skills at existing ones. On the other hand, acquiring an advantage by becoming better at existing procedures makes experimenting with brand new ones less attractive.

Suddenly, being a business looks quite difficult: what is good in the long run, March observed, is not always good in the short term. What is good at one moment in history is not always good at another.

> ❝ It is clear that exploration of new alternatives reduces the speed with which skills at existing ones are improved. It is also clear that improvements in competence at existing procedures make experimentation with others less attractive. ❞
>
> James G. March, "Exploration and Exploitation in Organizational Learning"

What is good even for one part of an organization is not always good for the other parts.

So, too, does the case for doing original research, or "exploration," at all. Pure research has less certain outcomes, longer time horizons to payoffs, and more diffuse benefits than simple product development. This is true, too, for new ideas, markets, and relationships with other organizations.

Each increase in competence makes innovation less attractive. March stated that competence in an inferior activity can become so great as to exclude other, much more profitable activities in an area where a business has little experience. Companies pursuing exploitation, therefore, can end up in sub-optimal equilibria.*

The question, March suggested, is one of balance. His goal, then, was to construct models to capture some of the considerations companies face in making decisions between exploring and exploiting. There is a second balancing act, too, between sustaining exploration, while also pursuing the adaptive processes that tend to inhibit it.

It is these models that March tried to provide in "Exploration and Exploitation in Organizational Learning." He asked first, how can organizations identify and understand what contributes to the optimal balance between exploring and exploiting. Second, and having found what an ideal balance looks like between these two, is there an ideal rate of turnover in employees, and could a business actually be better off having a mix between fast and slow learners?

These are the core questions of "Exploration and Exploitation in Organizational Learning."

The Participants

The first and overarching participants in "Exploration and Exploitation in Organizational Learning," as well as much of March's subsequent work, do not even come in for explicit mention. They are the economists who model firms as rational actors bestowed with perfect information and use complex mathematical models to investigate ways they will behave. According to theorists in the rational choice tradition, businesses can be assumed to act like individuals, and both will always make decisions that will maximize their individual self-interest.* Having made these simplifying assumptions, it is possible then to create formal models* that can be solved to identify stable equilibrium* states where no one can gain by changing their behavior. (The technical term for such states is a Nash equilibrium.*) Coase's neoclassical theory of the firm could be considered an example of this approach.

Rather than describing humans, this overly-simplified view more accurately described *Homo economicus,** said March and other critics: that is, an omniscient but pathological actor who knows no motive other than self-interest. (Game theorists, in turn, would say that using these simplifying assumptions allows them to come up with counterintuitive results, and assuming actors rationally pursue certain goals doesn't mean these goals necessarily need to be selfish ones.)

Prior to March, other scholars had thought of other ways to add depth to the neoclassical economists' abstract *Homo economicus* and their equally simplified view of businesses.

One writer, whose work March drew on significantly, is William Whyte,* an author (rather than an academic economist) who worked for twelve years for *Fortune* magazine. In his 1956 book *Organization Man*, Whyte drew an alternative model of individuals based on extensive interviews with US corporations like General Electric and Ford. Whyte found that employees are not rugged individuals (like *Homo economicus*), but instead believed organizations and groups could make better decisions than individuals. The American corporate employee, Whyte found, was actually meek and subscribed to an ethos of collectivism.

Other contemporary academics also figure in March's argument. Paul David,* an American economist at Stanford and Oxford working on the economics of scientific progress and technical change, provided him, for instance, with two of his crucial ideas. One is that the internal characteristics of firms induce them to follow a path of technological change. The other one is path dependence:* that decisions a firm has made in the past affect decisions it is making now.[1]

The Contemporary Debate

Contemporary debate in organization studies tends to follow two broad dimensions of controversy. One revolves around whether explanation should focus on top-down perspectives (sometimes called macro-primacy*), bottom-up ones (micro-primacy*), or other levels of analysis (such as everyday practice and routines, management, firms, or entire fields). Top-down approaches include looking at organizations through a lens of natural selection,* to explain which survive; bottom-up approaches include research focusing on the roles of individual managers, like decision theory* and strategic management.*

Another debate is between structure* and agency:* that is, how determined the behavior of individuals within an organization is. Those favoring structure emphasize the role of institutions in socializing individuals, while those who favor agency give more weight to the ability of individuals to act freely. Many researchers have argued one of these can be explained in terms of the other (normally, that agency can be entirely explained in terms of structure). Others have argued it is useful to be able to analyze organizations in terms of both.[2]

Finally, Coase's own neoclassical theory of the firm has been superseded by research in the tradition of mainstream economics. While he argued that firms come into being as a way of avoiding transaction costs, other scholars have pointed out there are transaction costs within businesses, while there are also forms of inter-firm cooperation that are part of a gradual continuum between firms and the deep waters of the market.[3] Other theories of the firm within the neoclassical economics tradition have taken its place, explaining the firm instead as a solution to other problems in mainstream economics, like collective action* or principal–agent* problems.

NOTES

1   Paul David, "Clio and the Economics of QWERTY," *American Economic Review* 75 (1985), 332-337.

2   Michael Reed, "In Praise of Duality and Dualism: Rethinking Agency and Structure in Organizational Analysis," *Organization Studies* Volume 18, Number 1, January 1, 1997, pp. 21-42.

3   George Barclay Richardson, "The Organisation of Industry," *The Economic Journal,* 1972, 82 (327): p. 883.

THE AUTHOR'S CONTRIBUTION

KEY POINTS

- March tried to show how the composition of the organization predisposes it towards exploiting or exploring.

- March used an approach of formal modeling, first developed in economics and then applied to social sciences.

- His study was part of the New Institutionalism, which looked at how institutions constrain and socialize individuals through rules, norms, and operating procedures.

Author's Aims

When he wrote "Exploration and Exploitation in Organizational Learning" in 1991, James March had already spent 38 years as an academic specializing in how organizations behave. His "Garbage Can" model of understanding how organizations make choices in 1972 (with Michael Cohen* and Johan Olsen*) had been influential, as had his first comparisons of business firms to political coalitions (in 1962), and explorations of bounded rationality (in 1978).

However, while he had looked at how organizations make decisions—as a political coalition of different parts, as a garbage can, in a boundedly-rational* way—he had only explored how organizations approach choices, not yet the subject of choice itself.

"Exploration and Exploitation in Organizational Learning," therefore, represented an important turning point in March's work. After building up an impressive set of concepts to explain how organizations make decisions, he then put them into play looking at a

❝ Exploration includes things captured by terms such as search, variation risk taking, experimentation, play, flexibility, discovery, innovation. Exploitation includes such things as refinement, choice, production, efficiency, selection, implementation, execution. ❞

James G. March, "Exploration and Exploitation in Organizational Learning"

problem he identified as pervasive within all businesses and other organizations that exist in other competitive environments.

March had another aim in view, though: he also suggested ways the internal composition of a business may be linked to its likely success either in exploring or exploiting. Instead of a neoclassical abstract business, he filled businesses with different compositions of fast learners and slow learners and different rates of turnover, and looked at how each sort of business did at exploiting old certainties or exploring new possibilities.

By using a framework that cut across all businesses in every society, March identified broad patterns linking how organizations learn, seek advantage, and make strategic decisions. While these sorts of universal observations also were an aim of the first generation of postwar research, he aimed to describe the nature of businesses, as well as linking their nature to how they behaved.

Approach

March's approach, in "Exploration and Exploitation in Organizational Learning," was to make models. Borrowing methods first established within economics, modeling in social science began in the 1950s, initially in political science. (*An Economic Theory of Democracy*, by Anthony Downs,* is probably the first example.[1]) Modeling, as an approach, starts with assumptions, which it then normally attempts to express in mathematical form. It then delves into the mathematics to produce an empirically testable proposition or several.

So why would one ever do this? One answer is that formulating an argument in terms of mathematics forces precision in the terms of the argument.[2] We can only express concepts in mathematical form (or express them "formally," in what is then called a "formal model"*) if we have engaged in careful thinking about the precise sense in which we wish to use it. It also forces us to be clear about which assumptions we have made. Just as concepts may have more than one meaning in ordinary speech, so likewise verbal arguments might include imprecise or missing assumptions in a way that would become painfully obvious in an attempt to render them formally.

Also, while it may take some time after reading a verbal argument to decide whether its arguments are valid or invalid—that is, whether its conclusion follows given the definitions and assumptions—it is very easy to check formal models for their logical validity (at least, once you understand the mathematics).

Finally, formal models make it possible to work through counterintuitive and unexpected results implied by the assumptions and definitions—to "bleed a set of assumptions dry, so to speak."[3]

Contribution in Context

March's approach in "Exploration and Exploitation in Organizational Learning" also drew heavily on the ideas of the New Institutionalism,* a movement in which he was a leading contributor.

The postwar behavioral revolution that dominated social science in the 1950s and 1960s, led in political science by the work of figures like Robert Dahl* and Philip Converse,* stressed studying individual and group behavior in systematic and scientific ways. In doing this, they were rebelling against a former mode of scholarship about politics that stressed studying institutions and interpretation of legal texts.

In the late 1960s and early 1970s, scholars like William Riker* and his students at the University of Rochester came to feel that more formal theoretic structure was required to make sense of the masses of data collected in the first two decades of behaviorism. They turned to theories of individual behavior from microeconomics* and game theory* techniques to find equilibrium* states where all actors had simultaneously maximized their self-interest.

The idea behind this project of formal modeling was twofold. First, if the actors and their interests were correctly specified, these equilibrium states would identify frequent patterns observable in actual political life. Second, the shared underlying mathematics behind all these models would make it easier to satisfy the broader behavioral aims of identifying universal scientific patterns underlying different areas of social science, and connecting them.

For March, an institution is a relatively enduring collection of rules and organized practices.[4] He considered institutions carriers of identities and roles, and that they create elements of order and predictability by fashioning, enabling, and constraining the individuals within them. With the New Institutionalism of which March's work forms a part, the study of social behavior had come full circle. From an interwar focus on formal institutions in legal terms that came to be seen as unpalatably old-fashioned, and then to a scientific focus on the individual to penetrate the formal surface of institutions and explain how behavior really works, it returned to looking at how institutionalized rules, norms, and operating procedures impact individual behavior.

NOTES

1   Anthony Downs, *An Economic Theory of Democracy*, (New York: Harper, 1957).

2   Morris P Fiorina, "Formal Models in Political Science," *American Journal of Political Science* XIX, no. 1, (1975): 133-159.

3   Fiorina, 137.

4   James G March and Johan Olsen, "The New Institutionalism: Organizational Factors in Political Life," *American Political Science Review* 78, no. 3, (1984): 734-749.

SECTION 2
IDEAS

MAIN IDEAS

KEY POINTS

- March argued that organizations are capable of learning by holding knowledge in their procedures, norms, rules, and forms: he calls these an "organizational code."

- Organizations also have different groups with different interests, knowledge, goals, and agendas.

- An organization with a mix of slow and quick learning individuals will always beat one where all members learn at the same rate.

Key Themes

The key themes of James March's "Exploration and Exploitation in Organizational Learning" are exploration and exploitation. Exploration, for an organization, means using the organization's scarce resources to develop new possibilities; exploitation means devoting these resources instead to pursuing greater efficiencies, increasing its members' skills and thereby the speed of the organization's processes. Both of these options clearly require organizations to be capable of learning.

How organizations hold and acquire knowledge was a key theme of March's. Learning, for an organization means both retaining and improving productivity, innovation, and competitive advantage. March argued that organizations hold knowledge in their "procedures, norms, rules, and forms," which collectively he called an "organizational code."[1] Learning then means improving this code: the company's procedures that constitute, effectively, its memory banks. The organizational code functions as the central repository of normative beliefs and practices.

> **❝** Organizations store knowledge in their procedures, norms, rules, and forms. They accumulate such knowledge over time, learning from their members. At the same time, individuals in an organization are socialized to organizational beliefs. **❞**
>
> James G. March, "Exploration and Exploitation in Organizational Learning"

If learning by improving their procedures and rules is something organizations can do, March also had important arguments about what organizations are. Businesses and other organizations, for him, are coalitions.[2] Thinking of a company as expressing the preferences, decisions, and information of its CEO alone is about as unreliable as thinking of the United States' government as acting solely in accordance with the decisions of its president. While presidents may wish this to be the case, there are many other points of considerable influence, including two other branches of the federal government, a professional career civil service in its own branch, and independent state governments, to begin with.

Similarly, businesses may (and probably do) subsume distinct preferences in their labor and management, in staff engaged with research and employees charged with production, between headquarters operations and ones based elsewhere, between older and younger employees, and between their executives and the members of their boards. "The business organization is properly viewed as a political system," March said in another work devoted wholly to this subject.[3] Like participants in a political system, experienced members of a business will engage in strategic behavior against people from elsewhere in their organization. March called "self-interested manipulation of information" (that is, lying, to put too fine a point on it) "a palpable feature of organizational life."[4]

Exploring the Ideas

March therefore depicted businesses and other organizations as complex systems, with diverse parts possessing different preferences and information. These systems also, collectively, can record lessons from experience. For their part, members of the organization both learn from and contribute to this central repository of institutional memory.

Individuals within an organization learn from its processes, norms, rules, and code: this is socialization, and it has the effect of raising the level of skill and efficiency of the average employee. At the same time, the organization's code itself is also capable of updating and learning from individuals whose beliefs mirror reality more closely than the organization's own procedures. March thought of turnover within the organization as responsible for updating its code: when new people enter it, the organization then has an opportunity to update its code to better reflect the world. At the same time, high turnover will *decrease* the average socialization time for all employees, and cause the average individual knowledge to decline.

March derived several implications from these observations. Quick-learning employees are good for individual knowledge (they will absorb lessons faster from the code), but bad for the organizational code itself. (Quick learners are faster to converge quickly on new received wisdom, which may in fact be wrong. Slower learners, though, will retain more organizational memory, and be less distracted by fads and incorrect new lessons.) A company with a mixture of slow- and quick-learning individuals, March said, will always beat one with a homogenous set of middling individuals. Such a company will have some quick-learning employees to observe new lessons from the world, while slow-learning employees better retain the lessons already encoded in the institution's memory.

Meanwhile, organizations composed of members with different types of information are unlikely all to subscribe to a common objective—such as maximizing long-run expected profits. While assuming profit-maximizing as a goal for all businesses is convenient for constructing economic theories, it is "almost certainly wrong as a micro-description of a business firm," said March.[5]

Language and Expression

March's prose is always clear, often witty, frequently deprecating or benevolent, and sometimes gracious. In a collection of papers he published three years before, he began his acknowledgements with: "The papers reprinted here are products of drinking wine with friends" and then began to list many of his colleagues in his discipline.[6]

In a 2006 keynote address in Norway, while summing up the field of organization studies he helped create, he called them simply "the impression of an affectionate enthusiast."[7] His self-deprecation was entirely typical when he addressed a room saying, "I learned early to be skeptical about the words of aged scholars. Now that I have become one of them, I am even more skeptical."[8]

Another noteworthy stylistic characteristic of March's is his breadth of reading and citations, reflecting a well-lived academic life, from his postgraduate work at Yale through to his work helping create a new field in stitching together disciplinary boundaries. This also extends, through frequent collaborations with Danish academic Johan Olsen,* to academic work done outside the United States, particularly in Scandinavia. March has spoken of his awareness that the dominance of US scholarship in the 1950s and 1960 was an artifact of World War II: from which the United States experienced a faster postwar economic recovery, and which caused an extraordinary immigration of scholars to North America from Europe. European scholarship, however, again came into its own in the 1970s and 1980s, and March stayed conversant with this new research and its slightly different preoccupations, where many US academics have instead only focused on American academic work.

NOTES

1   James G. March, "Exploration and Exploitation in Organizational Learning," *Organization Science* 2, no. 1 (1991): 73.

2   James G. March, "The Business Firm as a Political Coalition," *The Journal of Politics* 24, no. 4, (1962): 662-678.

3   March, "The Business Firm as a Political Coalition," 663.

4   James G. March, *Decision and Organizations*, (Oxford: Basil Blackwell, 1998), 6.

5   March, "The Business Firm as a Political Coalition," 669.

6   March, *Decision and Organizations*, acknowledgements.

7   James G. March, "The Study of Organizations and Organizing Since 1945," *Organization Studies* 28, no. 9, (2007): 9.

8   March, "The Study of Organizations and Organizing Since 1945," 9.

SECONDARY IDEAS

KEY POINTS

- Both individuals and organizations exercise "bounded rationality": they use shortcuts in making choices, and aspire to make "good enough" choices, not perfect ones.

- Diverse organizations are better at exploring; ones heavily socialized into an organization's rulebook excel at exploiting.

- Individuals can learn things within organizations they would struggle to learn on their own.

Other Ideas

James March in "Exploration and Exploitation in Organizational Learning" put forth a view of individuals and companies making decisions with bounded rationality.

Most researchers in the tradition of mainstream economics think of individuals and companies as acting with perfect information, and pursuing predetermined aims rationally.

However, bounded rationality is the idea, which March borrowed from his frequent coauthor Herbert Simon,* that decision-making is not perfectly rational, whether by individuals or organizations. Instead, choice is limited by the cognitive limitations of human minds, the tractability of the decision problem itself, and the time available to reach a decision. Bounded rationality is closely linked with the idea of "satisficing": people making decisions aspire to optimal solutions given the time and information available. They do not aim for the perfect ones that might be reached with perfect information and unlimited computational ability.

❝ In this spirit, for example, it has been argued that the persistence of garbage-can decision processes in organizations is related to the diversity advantage they provide in a world of relativity unstable environments.... ❞
James G. March, "Exploration and Exploitation in Organizational Learning"

March called bounded rationality—which might use mental shortcuts (called heuristics*)—an "accurate portrayal of much choice behavior and ... a normatively sensible adjustment to the costs and character of information gathering and processing."[1] He cited French philosopher Albert Camus* in support of his view that humans, he said, are not smart enough to be rational.[2]

Another direction March also delved into was the unexpected consequences produced by his model of organizational learning. One rather surprising result was rapid learning is not always desirable.[3] A code "can learn only from individuals who deviate it," said March, so slow learning will maintain diversity within the organization longer, thereby enabling the exploration that allows the knowledge in the organizational code to improve.[4]

Exploring the Ideas

Diversity suits exploration; socialization (and conformity), exploitation. An organization with huge diversity in its makeup is well fitted out for exploration; variation, in March's framework, is, after all, the key to evolutionary process. A heavily trained and socialized workforce will also lack variation that could serve as a basis for adaptation when an organization's environment changes.

Exploitation, on the other hand, is about making best use of what we already know. A workforce more heavily socialized into the organization's code—whose reason for existing is as a mechanism for best-practice transfer and vicarious learning—will better avoid mistakes made in the past, and achieve the organization's ends more quickly and cheaply.

A benefit of modeling, discussed previously, is producing counterintuitive results. March's "Exploration and Exploitation in Organizational Learning" provides several good examples of these. One finding that was already mentioned is that an organization benefits from having slow learners who help maintain the diversity needed for exploration and innovation. Another counterintuitive finding is that fast learning leads to more exploitative, not exploratory, behavior, because it drives out alternatives faster and so limits variation.

Similarly, while it may be intuitive to imagine that staff turnover imposes only costs to businesses—in recruitment, training, and loss of expertise—March's models instead showed a moderate level of turnover enormously benefited an organization, by mitigating the conformity introduced by members being educated into its code of beliefs. If a workforce has been socialized into the organizational code, new employees can reintroduce diversity, thereby increasing exploration and, as a consequence, knowledge.

The trick for any organization, therefore, lies in finding a mix, according to March. Organizations need to find an intermediate point where there is enough socialization into the organization's code to allow exploitation, but enough variation to allow exploration, too. Variation can come from turnover, or from a difference in learning rate: slow learners, said March, stay deviant long enough for the code to learn from them. Organizations tend to focus on exploitation to the detriment of exploration; but too much experimentation is as bad as none at all: organizations that only explore make no use of prior knowledge.

Overloaded
March's work on exploration and exploitation is widely known and has become a cornerstone of how we understand organizations, but

there are still parts of his research that seldom attract as much attention as they deserve.

One of these is March's finding that within an organization individuals can learn things they would struggle to learn on their own. March's model of learning has consequences for the individuals involved, not just for the organization as a whole. Though people often assume organizations must by their nature be less intelligent than individuals, March showed routines, standard operating procedures, and other components of organization's codes allow vicarious learning to permit members of organizations to learn in ways other than through direct experience.

Overlooked as well among March's other arguments are the points of dialogue he drew between his arguments in "Exploration and Exploitation in Organizational Learning" and other conversations about organizations.

For one, March's work largely was a response to prior reductionist scholarship on organizations reflecting in the work of Coase. Coase's theory of the firm suggests firms come to exist as a way of diminishing transaction costs. March's model suggested another alternative: if operating procedures, rules, and other aspects of organizational codes form a sort of memory tape recording the lessons of experience, if not the experiences themselves, then firms could as easily come to exist as ways of accumulating and sharing information over time.

Similarly, March identified that organizations' survival depends on there being diversity within its members: without it, they cannot adapt to changing environments, nor can they explore. The garbage can model for organizational choice acquires a new salience here, too: if being a garbage can expands the diversity internal to an organization, and helps its chances of successful exploration or adaptation, then organizations now have incentives to behave as garbage cans.

NOTES

1   James G. March, "Bounded Rationality, Ambiguity, and the Engineering of Choice," *The Bell Journal of Economics* 9, no. 2, (1978): 589.

2   Albert Camus, *L'Homme Révolte*, (Paris: Gallimard, 1951). (Published in English as *The Rebel*.)

3   James G. March, "Exploration and Exploitation in Organizational Learning," *Organizational Science* 2, no. 1, (1991): 75.

4   James G. March, "Exploration and Exploitation in Organizational learning," 76.

MODULE 7
ACHIEVEMENT

KEY POINTS

- Organizations themselves are capable of learning, with routines, processes, and other aspects of their operations serving as a memory tape.

- March systematized insights into organizational research, including bounded rationality and realization that organizations must either choose to innovate or increase efficiencies.

- March demonstrated that insights into corporate behavior can be drawn from economics, political science, and psychology, and combined in novel ways.

Assessing the Argument

In "Exploration and Exploitation in Organizational Learning," James March cleverly drew attention to, and also modeled, ways that learning occurs not only at the individual level, but also at the level of the organization. Furthermore, there is not only learning *within* organizations (by individuals), but also learning *by* organizations. For March, interpersonal learning within an organization was mediated by organizational codes that provide the memory mechanism by which organizations themselves learn.

These arguments make March's study justifiably a classic work. He provided a simple, provocative argument that produced counterintuitive results (innovation depends on having slow learners in your organization), and it also lent itself to expansion by other authors who were curious how introducing other features to March's models affected the results.

> ❝ But it may be instructive to reconfirm some elements of folk wisdom asserting that the returns to fast learning are not all positive, that rapid socialization may hurt the socializers even as it helps the socialized, that the development of knowledge may depend on maintaining an influx of the naive and ignorant, and that competitive victory does not reliably go to the properly educated. ❞
>
> James G. March, "Exploration and Exploitation in Organizational Learning"

Much of March's achievement here lay in systematizing and combining aspects of organizational behavior that other work (often, his) had drawn attention to before. Exploration and exploitation had previously been identified by Argyris and Schön as distinct options an organization might choose to pursue.[1] March and Cyert, in *A Behavioral Theory of the Firm,* already had outlined that firms do not try to maximize a particular measure such as profits, sales, or market share, but instead "satisfice" around goals set in a political process by constituencies within them.[2] Herbert Simon had already explored bounded rationality.[3]

March's contribution in "Exploration and Exploitation in Organizational Learning" consisted of combining these concepts, stripping them down to mathematical simplicity, and exploring how they play out together. Not only did his work give a greater airing to these concepts that had been individually explored previously, but it showed that together they were capable of generating unforeseen predictions.

Achievement in Context

Before "Exploration and Exploitation in Organizational Learning" and March's other work on the subject, neoclassical economists had assumed businesses maximized profits, enjoyed perfect information, and were internally unified (which is to say, they did not suffer from internal problems about allocating knowledge and other resources). They justified these assumptions because of the power of the models that, using them, they could erect.

March shattered this view. For one, he demonstrated that real firms encompass a number of separate groups (managers, stockholders, workers, members of the board). For another, these groups, which essentially are political coalitions, must now choose between a number of goals any of which could be taken to constitute business success (production, inventory, market share, sales, profits). Next, they must furthermore choose between pursuing these goals through exploitation or exploration. Finally, rather than solving how best to do this with near-perfect information and vast computational ability, they satisfice, use rule-of-thumb heuristics, and act within the constraints of bounded rationality.

While researchers working in the tradition of mainstream economics would not dispute much of this, they would have argued that construction of powerful models required assuming in each case to the contrary. March showed, in "Exploration and Exploitation in Organizational Learning," that equally powerful models can be created from a collection of assumptions that more closely correspond to how empirical research shows firms actually behaved.

In this, he helped to found a new discipline of organizational studies, which takes its modeling methods from economics, but also refined them using small-group insights from sociology, bargaining behavior from political science, and benefiting from research in psychology on cognitive limits and how individuals actually make decisions.

When March wrote "Exploration and Exploitation in Organizational Learning," it was a critical moment in the history of organizational studies, which was breaking away from its founding disciplines, and acquiring journals such as *Organization Studies,* (which in 1991 was in only its second year), professional bodies such as the European Group for Organizational Studies, and specialized academic departments such as the Work and Organization Studies Group at the MIT Sloan School of Management, and others at the University of Michigan, the University of Sydney, and European faculties such as at the University of Innsbruck.

Limitations

Models simplify, and March's in "Exploration and Exploitation in Organizational Learning" are no different. For March, all individuals have equal access to an organization's code. This access is independent, for example, of location: the spatial placement of individuals is irrelevant in his model. Although what if face-to-face interaction was critical to knowledge transfer; or what if people have a propensity to search for new knowledge near where they have obtained useful knowledge in the past?[4]

Other researchers have attempted to add in these considerations, and model how they might affect his results. Robert Axelrod* has added a spatial dimension to March's model, which placed 100 individuals on a 10x10 grid.[5] Learning only from proximate members slows the diffusion of knowledge through an organization, a result that is also mirrored in empirical research. Even trivial increases in the distances between colleagues, from 10 to 50 meters, dramatically lowers the probability of collaborations in laboratories devoted to research and development, a result that has been called the Allen curve.*[6]

Sometimes, though, incorporating these new dimensions produces results that actually fit with March's initial intuitions. One possibility, which is discussed by Cyert and March, is that search often begins as local and only becomes more distant if initial efforts fail to come up with a satisficing outcome.[7] Modeling this shows poor performers are more likely than strong ones to benefit from distant search, a factor which facilitates spread of knowledge across an organization.[8] (This shows slow learners are important in an organization, not only for exploration but also, when spatial considerations are introduced, for exploitation too.)

NOTES

1   Chris Argyris and Donald Schön, *Theory in Practice: Increasing Professional Effectiveness*, (San Francisco: Jossey-Bass, 1974).

2   Richard M. Cyert and James G. March, *A Behavioral Theory of the Firm,* (1963), 2nd ed. (Oxford: Blackwell Publishers, 1992).

3   Herbert Simon, "A Behavioral Model of Rational Choice," *The Quarterly Journal of Economics* 69, no. 1, (1955): 99–118.

4   Kent Miller et al, "Adding Interpersonal Learning and Tacit Knowledge to March's Exploration-Exploitation Model," *The Academy of Management Journal* 49, no. 4 (2006): 711.

5   Robert Axelrod, "The Dissemination of Culture: A Model with Local Convergence and Global Polarization," *Journal of Conflict Resolution,* (1997).

6   Thomas J. Allen, *Managing the Flow of Technology*, Cambridge, Massachusetts: MIT Press, 1977.

7   Cyert and March, *A Behavioral Theory of the Firm.*

8   Daniel Levinthal, "Adaptation on Rugged Landscapes," *Journal of Management Science* 43, no. 7, (1997): 934-950.

MODULE 8
PLACE IN THE AUTHOR'S WORK

KEY POINTS

- March helped to create a new field of organization studies by working with experts from diverse fields. He took insights from each of their disciplines and combined them into his models.

- Social science disciplines and business schools in the US became more professionalized in the postwar period, providing a supporting environment for the study of organizations to do so as well.

- March's thinking reminds us that businesses are chaotic organizations that innovate only with difficulty, and can learn the wrong lessons in quickly changing environments.

Positioning

In "Exploration and Exploitation in Organizational Learning," James March saw himself as stitching together a new field, to study organizations and how they behave, while drawing insights from across the social science disciplines, and using relevant work in one to remedy what he saw as deficiencies in others. For example, he borrowed from psychology its cognitive work on decision-making, to complement the highly abstract, unrealistic nature of much modeling work in economics.

Not surprisingly, March is a great collaborator, and many of the other works for which he is known are collaborations. These include significant works jointly with Norwegian political scientist Johan Olsen, economist (and later, university president) Richard Cyert, and

❝ Old-timers, on average, know more, but what they know is redundant with knowledge already reflected in the code...Novices know less on average, but what they know is less redundant with the code and occasionally better, thus more likely to contribute to improving the code. ❞

James G. March, "Exploration and Exploitation in Organizational Learning"

polymath Herbert Simon (who received the Nobel Memorial Prize in Economic Sciences, as well as the Turing Award in computing).

With Simon, March painted a picture of a problem-solving individual in an organization who can only do a few things, or one, at a time, and can only attend to a small part of the information on offer. (If this image bears a great deal of similarities with the flowchart of a computer with limited memory processing tasks, remember that Simon was a pioneer in artificial intelligence.) A routine that allocates tasks among roles is efficient if it gives this person complementary decisions to make over time. This book, *Organizations*, also says an organization that relates promotion to some index of productivity will outperform one that essentially rewards seniority. Expectations of vertical mobility make individuals identify with an organization more, and to feel similarities with their subordinates and superiors.[1]

With Cyert, the university administrator, March examined the actual processes in which businesses make decisions. In this book, *A Behavioral Theory of the Firm*, decision-making processes have a starring role, beginning with negotiating the business's very goals.[2] Since coalition members span the gamut from customers, government regulators, stockholders, and managers and workers, these goals will not necessarily be consistent. Becoming compliant with a new regulation or keeping customers happy does not slot nicely into maximizing profit, but a business does not have the luxury of picking and choosing. Meanwhile agreements made over task allocation and budgets are institutionalized into semi-permanent arrangements.

In a long succession of joint work with political scientist Olsen, March developed the Garbage Can model, and helped reintroduce institutions (through the New Institutionalism) to a political science field that had moved away from them a generation before as reflecting a fusty, old fashioned, legal-formulistic turn of scholarship.

Integration

The origin of systematization of organization studies as a field in its own right took place at the same time as business schools underwent a revolution, in the 1960s in North America and afterward in Europe, to become more academic and research-oriented.

This story began in 1965, when Rand McNally published an influential *Handbook of Organizations*.[3] At the time of its publication, it was possibly the most useful review of the then state of knowledge about organizations for researchers interested in insights and work in other disciplines. (At the same time, so new was the field that one contemporary review wonders "if the book find[s] its way to the executive's bookshelf, it will be used for more than decorative purposes."[4]) This work partly offers a snapshot of people working in the new field. Generally speaking, they were based—60 per cent of them—in traditional social science departments. They were young— two-thirds of them under 40. Their formative years accordingly were a time of the professionalization of behavioral social science in the postwar United States. Techniques for the gathering and multivariate analysis were taking hold, as quantitative social science in its new, scientific incarnation came to be included as a division of the National Science Foundation, and the first social scientists were elected to the National Academy of Science. The *Handbook*'s editor, coincidentally, was a young James March.[5]

The key themes in "Exploration and Exploitation in Organizational

Learning"—how unwieldy organizations learn by encoding inferences from history into routines that guide behavior, and then make decisions under constraints of time, rationality, and information—continued to be the predominant themes in March's lifelong research.

If organization studies has grown more professional, so also have businesses, including in the ways they gather information and make decisions. March considered this more recently in a 2006 scholarly article on "Rationality, Foolishness, and Adaptive Intelligence."[6] Unsurprisingly, for a researcher whose consistent theme has been the chaotic nature of businesses and the way in which they make decisions, March thought this development may easily do as much harm as good. The lesson that seemingly intelligent learning can lead organizations astray seems never far from his lips, through competency traps or faddishness. Repeating a familiar theme from "Exploration and Exploitation in Organizational Learning," March said organizations' survival "may also be served by the heroism of fools and the blindness of true believers," and their imperviousness to feedback "is both the despair of adaptive intelligence and, conceivably, its salvation."

Significance

Much of the significance of March's arguments in "Exploration and Exploitation in Organizational Learning" lies in the way they examine decision-making under conditions of inconsistent, ill-defined preferences, coupled with a shifting involvement of members of an organization in decision-making roles.

At a time when rationalized large corporations appear increasingly to dominate both economic life and spatial organization—and the main thoroughfares of most cities, increasingly in most countries, feature similarly organized franchises of worldwide fast-food restaurants, supermarkets, and fuel companies—March reminds us (and them) that businesses still are organized anarchies. As the world grows more complex, less stable, and less understood, for all their pretenses of rationalization, the largest companies remain constrained in their choices by the cognitive and attention limits of decision-makers.

March's work, in "Exploration and Exploitation in Organizational Learning," turned large organizations on their head: in the Garbage Can model as well as *Behavioral Theory of the Firm*, organizations are collections of choices looking for problems; issues and feelings looking for decision situations in which they might be aired; solutions looking for issues to which they might be the answer; and decision makers (including, now, professional management consultants) looking for work.[7]

The result somewhat is to topple large, professional, corporate governance from its throne. Not only is the way in which businesses arrive at decisions messy (and the businesses, themselves, are also messy), but in a rapidly changing environment, we should not underestimate how difficult it is for organizations to learn to do anything useful, and how easy it is instead to learn the wrong lessons amidst a rapidly changing environment and bounded rationality.

NOTES

1   James March and Herbert Simon, *Organizations*, (New York: John Wiley and Sons, 1958).

2   Richard M. Cyert and James G. March, *A Behavioral Theory of the Firm,* (1963), 2nd ed. (Oxford: Blackwell Publishers, 1992).

3   James March, ed., *Handbook of Organizations,* (Chicago: Rand McNally, 1965).

4   Charles Bonjean, "Handbook of Organizations (Review)", *Social Forces* 45, no. 3, (1967): 445-446.

5   March, ed., *Handbook of Organizations*.

6   James March, "Rationality, Foolishness, and Adaptive Intelligence," *Strategic Management Journal* 27, (2006): 201-214.

7   Michael D. Cohen et al, "A Garbage Can Model of Organizational Choice," *Administrative Science Quarterly* 17, no. 1, (1972): 2.

SECTION 3
IMPACT

MODULE 9
THE FIRST RESPONSES

KEY POINTS

- March's model has been attacked as simplistic and lacking backing from empirical data.

- March himself has been labelled as broad-brush and provocative, leaving to others both thinking through the consequences of his frameworks and conducting the research to verify it.

- Critics have asked what the field of organizational studies seeks to explain: the way organizations learn, the outcomes of the learning, or the forms that learning can take.

Criticism

Published in 1991, James March's "Exploration and Exploitation in Organizational Learning" was a slow-burn success, having received no citations at all in the year after it appeared (1992). Cited only a small number of times in each of 1993, 1994, and 1995, suddenly in 1996 it was cited more than 30 times, then 100 times in 2003. Its citations then skyrocketed: 240 in 2007, then 320 in 2010, next 420 in 2011, and 540 in 2015 by which time it had arrived at the stature of an academic blockbuster.[1] Partly this reflected the steadily growing audience for this new field of organizational studies, as well as the number of people working in it.

Mikael Holmqvist* and other researchers noted the simplicity of model of organizational learning as well as its lack of empirical data.[2] According to Holmqvist, March's work "acknowledged these dynamics" between exploitation and exploration, "but it has not

" Reason inhibits foolishness: learning and imitation inhibit experimentation. "

James G. March, "Exploration and Exploitation in Organizational Learning"

investigated *how* they occur, that is, according to what key organizational mechanisms."[3] In time, the general nature of its insight and framework into collective learning under ambiguous conditions became a strength. It provided a starting point for other researchers either to undertake empirical work, or to append their own "plug and play" additions on to March's framework, to observe how doing so would change its predictions.

Others, like Richard Langlois*, though praising the Carnegie school's emphasis on "looking inside the black box of decision-making," noted the niche nature of organization studies when viewed from the more established academic disciplines. "It should not be surprising ... that the Carnegie approach has had little resonance within the halls of economics—and almost none within its inner sanctums."[4] This, by the way, is not *entirely* the case—at the time he wrote "Exploration and Exploitation in Organizational Learning," March had actually been cited 302 times in social sciences journals, though ever so slightly more in business (117), organizations (83), and sociology (71), while his inroads seem to have been a touch more limited in political science (34) and economics (27).[5]

Responses

March's concept of limited (or bounded) rationality has come in for praise. According to Douglas Price,* one reviewer, holding up information and time-constrained rationality as a normative ideal (as well as empirical assumption) provides hope for people with organizations in moving towards possible "satisfactory" goals rather

than unrealistically taxing maximizing ones.[6] Satisficing avoids one
extreme, the normative ideal of computer-like rationality based on an
encyclopedia-like data set, while meanwhile not going so far as to
view decision makers as incapable of rational thought or driven only
by irrational urges.[7]

Charles Stauffacher,* an executive, said March's pessimism about
organizations is not something he recognized from his own experience.
March "invests the process with greater mystery and elaborateness
than actually exists," he said, adding that "an involved description of
the human ability to recognize, select, identify, resort to, etc., goals leads
up to a prediction that an organization will have a budget—though
not so phrased."[8]

Lawrence Mohr,* one researcher responding to March's work
over his long career, characterized him as "provocative" and "[leaving]
us with the opportunity to do our own rethinking," casting
frameworks rather than conducting detailed empirical research
within them.[9] His aims appear to be more to breathe "vitality and
reality" into the field, and not so much "attempt to bring the major
ideas to a stage of detailed completeness and theoretical maturity."[10]

Partly this may be because March, like other people who started
new fields (Sigmund Freud* in psychoanalysis* might possibly come
to mind), is a dominant progenitor of a new scholarly area whose own
work consequently cannot always be read in complete isolation from
the new discipline as a whole. Anne Miner,* one reviewer, thus
compared him to a Greek chorus commenting on the field, with a
trace nonetheless of a contrarian spirit. His work, said the reviewer,
persistently points out "the lack of clothes on a variety of emperors,"
and "creates a sense of being in a conversation with someone who
persistently points to important things that somehow lie just outside of
our ordinary awareness."[11]

Conflict and Consensus

Organizational studies began as a heretical movement nailing its theses to the orthodoxy of neoclassical economics of the time, and has maintained that rebellious spirit. Not surprisingly, practitioners of mainstream economics have raised criticisms from time to time about the splinter church of organizational research. For one, if organizational studies is a social science, what is the dependent variable,* that is, what does it seek to explain? Is it the sources of organizational learning? Is it the outcomes of this learning? Or is it on the different forms learning could take? Perhaps, suggests one academic, it is all three.[12]

In the world of empirical business reality, an idea that has taken greater root in some areas than others—Silicon Valley,* say, more than corporate America—is March's recommendation that organizations should hire slow learners, a term which for one reader seems broad enough to include "deviants, heretics, eccentrics, crackpots, weirdos, and just plain original thinkers, even though they will come up with many ideas that are strange mutations, dead ends, and utter failures."[13]

One area of possible conflict simmering afoot derives from the fact organizational studies have doubtlessly benefited from the professionalism of business education, just as it has done from the increasingly scientific nature of social science research at North American and European universities. This professionalism is related to corporate largesse that funds students through part-time executive education programs in business schools, and supports particular pieces of research as well as faculty positions and research bodies as well.

This brings universities and business schools very close indeed to the world of business: something March has pushed back from. "Students are not customers," he wrote, and "teaching is not a job, it is a sacrament."[14] March has fought back against casting business school as just another actor in markets that supply educational courses to satisfy the demand of customers wealthy enough to pay for them. "A university is only incidentally a market," March argued, "It is more essentially a temple ... dedicated to knowledge and a human spirit of inquiry." [15]

NOTES

1   Johann Peter Murmann, "More Exploration and Less Exploitation," *Management and Organization Review* 13, no. 1, (2017): 5.

2   Mikael Holmqvist, "Experiential Learning Processes of Exploitation and Exploration within and Between Organizations: An Empirical Study of Product Development," *Organization Science* 15, no. 1 (2004): 70.

3   Holmqvist, "Experiential Learning Processes of Exploitation and Exploration Within and Between Organizations: An Empirical Study of Product Development," 80.

4   Richard N. Langlois, "The Economics of Choice, Change, and Organization," Review Essay, *Journal of Economic Literature* 42, no. 2 (2004): 507-8.

5   John F. Padgett, "Organizational Learning: Papers in Honor of (and by) James G. March (Review)," *Contemporary Sociology* 21, no. 6 (1992): 744-749.

6   Douglas Price, "Organizations: A Social Scientist's View," *Public Administration Review* 19, no. 2, (1959): 126-7.

7   Price, "Organizations," 126.

8   Charles Stauffacher, "Organizations: An Executive's View," *Public Administration Review*, Volume 19, no. 2, (1959): 124-5.

9   Lawrence B. Mohr, "Ambiguity and Choice in Organizations (Review)," *American Political Science Review*, 72, no. 3, (1978): 1033-1035.

10 Mohr, "Ambiguity and Choice in Organizations (Review)."

11 Anne Miner, "The Pursuit of Organizational Intelligence (Review)," *Administrative Science Quarterly* 47, no. 1, (2002): 174-178.

12 Martin Schultz, "Organizational Learning," in Joel Baum (ed), *Companion to Organizations*, (Blackwell Publishers, 2001).

13 Robert Sutton, *Weird Ideas That Work: 11 and 1/2 Practices for Promoting, Managing, and Sustaining Innovation*, (New York: The Free Press, 2002), 36.

14 James G. March, *The Pursuit of Organizational Intelligence,* (Malden, Mass.: Blackwell, 1999), 378.

15 March, *The Pursuit of Organizational Intelligence,* 378.

MODULE 10
THE EVOLVING DEBATE

KEY POINTS

- March's arguments have encouraged attempts to understand precisely how organizations learn.

- Scholars have focused both on how members of an organization might have localized knowledge that exists outside official boundaries, and on modelling how organizations learn through reinforcement.

- March's framework has been used to investigate the declining prevalence of renegades within government think tanks, how scientific disciplines learn, and how ethno-political organizations turn to crime.

Uses and Problems

One aspect of James March's "Exploration and Exploitation in Organizational Learning," which other researchers found especially interesting, is his idea that organizations are things that can learn and do so by drawing inferences from experience, and then encoding and recording these inferences into organizational rules, procedures, conventions, and strategies. Encoding knowledge in routines lets organizations retain, share, and re-use what has worked in the past.

The idea that organizations can learn has become a key point of differentiation between behaviorist organizational theory and ones from classical economics. Cyert and March's *Behavioral Theory of the Firm* envisages that there is a multi-level hierarchy of procedures: so, lower-level ones are changed in response to short-run feedback, whereas the higher-level procedures adapt less rapidly and guide how lower-level operating procedures change.[1] Another article explores

> ❝ Rapid socialization of individuals into the procedures and beliefs of an organization tends to reduce exploration. ❞
>
> James G. March, Exploration and Exploitation in Organizational Learning

routines as autonomous, disembodied imprints of history, capable of surviving turnover of the people who make and use them, recording history's lessons, but not the history itself, to organization members who have not themselves experienced it.[2]

But how does it all work? One direction of further work that has carried on out of March's ideas (and perpetuates much of his skepticism) has explored different possibilities, some of them highlighting optimism in just how organizations might learn, others quite the reverse.

It might work very badly indeed, retaining old lessons that are inappropriate for new situations, as one article explores.[3] When there are dedicated organizational agencies in charge of encoding, they tend to have limited resources and capacities: discontinuous, delayed, and incomplete mapping of lessons is what results.[4] Possibly, encoding valuable lessons in tangible depositories raises the risk of letting strategically important wisdom seep out to an organization's competitors, other authors suggest.[5] When an organization focuses too much on one particular existing competency, it can have a detrimental effect on the organization by hindering learning elsewhere. March and a coauthor call this a "competency trap.*"[6]

Other research has found smaller organizations update their routines more quickly than large ones; one article found smaller organizations created and shed job roles faster, adapting to changing environments by updating that part of the organizational routine that dealt with job roles. Large organizations lacked the monitoring and updating capacity to do this, suggesting in this, at least, that smaller organizations are nimbler, both at learning lessons and updating them.[7]

Schools of Thought

One scholar in the field, John Padgett,* suggests there are two main axes—one of them theoretical, the other substantive—to the schools of thought that have followed on from March's work in organizational learning.[8] The first axis charts whether the focus should be on understanding how individuals learn from the codes of organizations, or on the organization's codes and how these absorb and map experience. The second is on whether, in either case, the focus should be on adaptation or learning: is the modification of routines a fairly direct matter, occurring via trial, error, and selection, or is it fairly mediated, through cognitive representations?

At the individual level of analysis, Michael Cohen* and various coauthors make a strong case for "procedural memory"*—when members of an organization display much more skill and craft in hands-on behavior than they can explain verbally.[9] Others have explored how this "localized knowledge" by experienced employees might often even reside outside the boundaries of procedures that the organization sanctions officially.[10] This approach leads itself to genetic-evolutionary understandings of adaptation, where loosely coupled clusters of routines recombine and reproduce in a loose bricolage against dimly perceived, rugged landscapes.

Another school of research that hovers more at the level of the organization tries to derive insights about how groups behave from psychological research about reinforcement learning:* that is, actions that produce a positive outcome are used more often afterwards in the same situation (the "law of effect"*), and in future iterations it will take less time to solve a similar problem on the first trial (the "power law of practice"*). This approach has lent itself well to mathematical modeling (the models are often called varieties of

"Bush-Mosteller equations"*)[11]. Psychology has laid aside these approaches (associated there with the work of B. F. Skinner*); March, in *Exploitation versus Exploration*, suggests the avenue becomes far more interesting when applied to organizations as ecologies of learning, instead of individuals.

In Current Scholarship

Some scholarly arenas in which March's work in "Exploration and Exploitation in Organizational Learning" are applied are unsurprising.

March, whose work both identifies organizational codes and then gives such surprisingly sympathetic treatment to the "slow learners" in an organization who are resistant to adopting a new organizational orthodoxy, has fostered work on renegades and intellectual outliers.

One study, from 2015, looks at renegades within the RAND Corporation,* an independent research and analysis organization established in California in 1948 and frequently used in consultancy roles by US government agencies and the military in their postwar expansion.[12] The authors found that the number of intellectual mavericks within the organization thinned out, as RAND's confidence, endurance, and growth undermined variety.

Other uses may surprise slightly: March nearly always speaks in terms of organizations rather than only businesses, and so researchers have applied (in a 2015 work) his findings about exploration and exploitation to managing complex healthcare organizations.[13]

Students of academic disciplines have a particular affection for March's theory also, applying it in its broadest brushstrokes (also in research from 2015) to understanding scientific disciplines as organizations.[14] Others have used him in arguments about rethinking trends in the relationship between universities and the corporate world, and even in understanding how ethno-political* organizations, learning from opportunities in their environment, turn to crime.[15]

NOTES

1   Richard M. Cyert and James G. March, *A Behavioral Theory of the Firm,* (1963), 2nd ed. (Oxford: Blackwell Publishers, 1992).

2   Barbara Levitt and James G. March, "Organizational Learning," *Annual Review of Sociology* 14, (1988): 319-340.

3   William Barnett et al, "An Evolutionary Model of Organizational Performance," *Strategic Management Journal* 15, (1994): 11-28.

4   Martin Schulz, "Limits to Bureaucratic Growth: The Density Dependence of Organizational Rule Births," *Administrative Science Quarterly* 43, no. 4, (1998): 845-876.

5   Udo Zander and Bruce Kogut, "Knowledge and the Speed of the Transfer and Imitation of Organizational Capabilities: An Empirical Test," *Organization Science* 6, no. 1, (1995): 76-92.

6   Barbara Levitt and James G. March, "Organizational Learning," *Annual Review of Sociology* 14, (1988): 319-340.

7   Anne Miner, "Organizational Evolution and the Social Ecology of Jobs," *American Sociological Review* 56, (1991): 772–785.

8   John F. Padgett, "Learning from (and about) March," *Contemporary Sociology* 21, no. 6, (1992): 744.

9   Michael D. Cohen and Paul Bacdayan, "Organizational Routines are Stored as Procedural Memory: Evidence from a Laboratory Study," *Organization Science* 5, no. 4, (1994): 554–568.

10 John Seely Brown and Paul Duguid, *The Social Life of Information,* (Cambridge, Mass.: Harvard Business School Press, 2000).

11 Ido Erev and Alvin Roth, "Predicting How People Play Games: Reinforcement Learning in Experimental Games with Unique, Mixed Strategy Equilibria," *The American Economic Review* 88, no. 4, (1998): 848-881.

12 Mie Augier et al, "Perspective—The Flaring of Intellectual Outliers: An Organizational Interpretation of the Generation of Novelty in the RAND Corporation," *Organization Science* 26, no. 4, (2015): 1140-1161.

13 James Begun and Marcus Thygeson, "Managing Complex Healthcare Organizations," in Myron Fotler, Donna Malvey, and Donna Slovensky, *Handbook of Healthcare Management,* (Cheltenham, UK: Edward Elgar Publishing, 2015), 9.

14 Feng Shi et al, "Weaving the Fabric of Science: Dynamic Network Models of Science's Unfolding Structure," *Social Networks* 43, (2015): 73-85.

15 Thomas Sattelberger, "Rethinking Corporate Universities," *EFMD Insights into Executive Education and Workplace Learning* 2, Brussels: European Foundation for Management Development, (2015): 1-6.; Victor Asal et al, "Why do Ethnopolitical Organizations Turn to Crime?" *Global Crime* 16, no. 4, (2015): 306-327.

MODULE 11
IMPACT AND INFLUENCE TODAY

KEY POINTS

- March has had a vast impact both on academic research and broader public debate.

- His work on how organizations learn has prompted research into how companies can become better at learning.

- Digital disruption has made it more vital for companies to learn to be innovative, making March's lessons more timely than ever.

Position

Living as we do in a modern society of organizations, James March has suggested in "Exploration and Exploitation in Organizational Learning" that students of organizations confront two very different roles regarding their paradoxes.

The first is within modernity* as its technicians, providing advice to better manage organizations and individuals within them, addressing competing demands between exploitation and exploration and other paradoxes, all while accepting its tensions.

The second is as cultural interpreters of modernity, here being more attentive to its paradoxes, including the limits of human reason in the modernist quest for order and control.

Much of March's work is dedicated to a second aim, demonstrating the incompleteness of reason: this through "ambiguity and equivocality" as well as "irony, paradox, playfulness, and metaphor."[1] This is a theme that extends through his Garbage Can model, to the role of the "technology of foolishness" in exploration and innovation,

> **❝ But a major threat to the effectiveness of such learning is the possibility that individuals will adjust to an organizational code before the code can learn from them. ❞**
>
> James G. March, "Exploration and Exploitation in Organizational Learning"

to his filmography on the leadership style of Don Quixote. For March, this is not rhetorical frosting, but a serious attempt to draw attention to the ambiguities, contradictions, and paradoxes besetting large pervasive organizations that are disposed (with the help of management consultants and business schools) to depict themselves as highly rational, ordered, and efficient.

On the other hand, if people in organizations only exercise bounded rationality, then it is worth paying attention to the heuristics that they use to make decisions under constraint. Identifying and refining heuristics has become a promising direction of research. One influential book researching heuristics sounds quite close to March in this advice: "if a competitor is using a slow procedure to find the exact solution, you may be able to discover some inexact but useful solution before they do."[2]

Interaction

From a practitioner's perspective, March's work on how organizations learn has provoked thought about why companies struggle to become or remain learning organizations.[3]

Organizations are more likely to learn if their members have a mindset that seeks challenges and learning opportunities; by contrast, a mindset of avoiding failure at all costs limits the ability to learn, according to a professor of psychology at Stanford.[4]

Viewed from an academic perspective, James March's work, here and elsewhere, attempts to lay the basis for a new institutionalism. This new institutionalism is aimed at mainstream economics (and to a large extent, political science) research as practiced in the postwar period and its extreme emphasis on the individual. Among other things, March's new institutionalism offers to supplant a "logic of appropriateness" for the "logic of expected consequences" of economics.[5]

The New Institutionalism has been broadly cited and influential. It has suggested institutions might be a level of analysis as well as individuals, and that institutions' properties that do not simply reduce to the individual level. March's institutional scripts represent properties of the organization itself, not individuals.

Other aspects of institutions' New Institutionalism highlights include the mechanisms by which they generate incentives, monitoring, power and influence, participation, and organizational culture.

Not surprisingly, New Institutionalism has also attracted rejoinders from within economics and political science. One common rejoinder is that "the logics, far from being mutually excluding, overlap very considerably."[6] It remains a dissident approach within economics and political science, but has influenced those working with mainstream rational choice approaches to attempt to address its questions and concerns within their own paradigms.

The Continuing Debate

March's work provides important findings about how businesses can arrange themselves internally for innovation: through maintaining an intellectual diversity within an organization, (which he models as quick and fast learners), and ensuring that there is sufficient turnover that the organizational code continues to update.

How organizations can improve as innovators has attracted only more attention with the rise of new, digitally-based "disruptive" start-ups such as Uber.* (Those familiar with Joseph Schumpeter's ideas of creative disruption will find technology-based disruptive innovation a strangely familiar concept.) Uber, like other start-ups including AirBnB,* functions on a sharing economy* model in which the company itself provides an online marketplace, where people can sell spare capacity in assets they own; Uber does not own automobiles, and AirBnB does not own hotel rooms.

Where digital disruption has taken place, the effect on incumbent business operators, such as black cab drivers in London, has been vast. Other sectors, such as mining and fuel, have been unaffected. Still other sectors, such as the news media, have been in secular decline because of disruption by digital competitors.

The way in which organizations might aim to escape "competency traps" of the sort identified by March, and to innovate effectively in a marketplace characterized by far more rapid change than in previous decades, will only attract growing debate.

Angus Dawson,* a partner at McKinsey* who heads the organization's Strategy Practice, states "by far, the hardest thing for an established company to do, first of all, it to disrupt itself."[7]

NOTES

1   James G. March, *A Primer on Decision Making: How Decisions Happen*, (New York, NY: The Free Press, 1994), 211.

2   Zbigniew Michalewicz and David Fogel, *How to Solve It: Modern Heuristics*, 2nd ed., (Berlin: Springer, 2004).

3   Francesca Gino and Bradley Staats, "Why Organizations Don't Learn: Our Traditional Obsessions—Success, Taking Action, Fitting In, and Relying on Experts—Undermine Continuous Improvement," *Harvard Business Review* 93, no. 11 (2015): 110–118.

4   Carol S. Dweck, *Mindset*, (London: Hachette, 2017) (updated edition).

5 James G March and Johan Olsen, "The New Institutionalism: Organizational Factors in Political Life," *American Political Science Review* 78, no. 3, (1984): 734-749.

6 Kjell Goldmann, "Appropriateness and Consequences: The Logic of Neo-Institutionalism," *Governance* 18, no. 1, (2005): 35-52.

7 "Digital Strategy: Understanding the Economics of Disruption," *McKinsey Quarterly*, April 2016. Online at < https://www.mckinsey.com/business-functions/strategy-and-corporate-finance/our-insights/digital-strategy-understanding-the-economics-of-disruption> (accessed December 23, 2017).

MODULE 12
WHERE NEXT?

KEY POINTS

- As artificial intelligence redefines the role of humans in the workplace, March's ideas will become even more relevant.
- March's models hold important lessons for large corporations looking for ways to behave like small start-ups.
- Understanding March correctly is important, given how influential his ideas have become.

Future Directions

James March's "Exploration and Exploitation in Organizational Learning" takes readers on an important journey in several important directions of understanding organizations: how they reach decisions, trade-offs between pursuing innovation and efficiency, how they store lessons in operating procedures, and how they value (or otherwise) slow and other misfit workers.

Businesses and other established organizations are on the cusp of a period of unparalleled change. How organizations learn and adapt, it appears, will be more crucial in the coming decades than ever before.

The rise of machine learning in the workplace questions the role and future of humans at work entirely. With the coming rise of robotics and artificial intelligence in the workplace, uniquely human traits that an artificial mind cannot emulate, like emotional intelligence, creativity, persuasion, and innovation, will become more valuable. Certainly, the role of humans in the workplace will be different. The challenges for organizations to adapt will be vast.

"[Rapid] learning is not always desirable. "
James G. March, "Exploration and Exploitation in Organizational Learning"

By 2050, the United Nations* projects the world's urban population will have increased by 72 percent. In the slightly nearer term, by 2030 demand for energy will have increased by 50 percent, and demand for water by 40 percent. The workplace itself is becoming more freelance, with 60 percent of people in the United Kingdom, United States, Germany, India, and China believing "few people will have stable, long-term employment in the future."[1] Meanwhile, the legacies of the 2008 global financial crisis,* and the failures it exposed in corporations as well as financial markets, continue to be unpacked.

In this context, both among researchers and in the public eye, March's voice of dissent and skepticism has provided an antidote and corrective to awed orthodoxies about how the public and researchers would think of corporations and their capacity for rational behavior, and how corporations would think of themselves. Moreover, how organizations learn is increasingly relevant for the future—and so will be conversations about how to manage it.

Potential
Among scholars, March's influence has been vast. "Exploration and Exploitation in Organizational Learning" has been cited by 19,726 scholarly works, according to Google Scholar. *A Behavioral Theory of the Firm* was cited by even more: 27,945.[2] His work with Herbert Simon, *Organizations*, received 25,948 citations.[3]

March attracted attention by framing broad questions (not all of which he attempted to answer definitively). He contributed insightful frameworks that inspired copious research by capturing, and continuing to capture, the curiosity of generations (now) of researchers. The questions he identified remain urgent ones and will continue to guide scholars.

March's relevance is even greater for businesses, which seek to grow in a corporate world. RAND's growth from a small research startup to a megalith with layers of administrators, meetings, and committees drove out ambitious intellectual renegades.[4] Whether through close relationships with incubators and accelerators, or founding "lab" units like Google and Amazon, or investing in and eventually acquiring smaller boutique companies, large companies are facing the dilemma of how to behave as nimbly as startups.

Against this backdrop, the Silicon Valley model is unfolding along lines very familiar to readers of "Exploration and Exploitation in Organizational Learning": innovation and exploration comes most naturally to little companies, efficiencies and exploitation to large ones.

March's lessons, about nurturing heterogeneous workforces and discouraging orthodoxies, whether groupthink or faddishness, remain only more relevant to large companies wanting to recapture an innovative spirit. Meanwhile, his findings about gaining efficiencies by paying attention to the organization's code, processes, and script, and the way information is shared among members of an organization, are vital to small, nimble start-ups, looking to be efficient.

Summary

James March's influence in "Exploration and Exploitation in Organizational Learning"—not only on understanding dilemmas about pursuing innovation versus efficiency, but also on the questions of how organizations learn, decide, and value maverick employees— is so vast as to be virtually incalculable. He has been, and remains, the most frequently read student of organizations at a time when the field of organizational studies was just gaining a foothold, and a highly visible public intellectual whose work transcended academic boundaries.

In an academic career that is not yet over, March wrote or edited 26 books and taught generations of researchers and thinkers during a highly influential 47-year tenure at Stanford, coupled with his formative earlier teaching years at the Carnegie Institute of Technology and the University of California, Irvine.

It must be admitted, it is the rare academic at a senior research university who, along with a highly cited body of scholarly work, has also created two films (on *Don Quixote* in 2003, and *War and Peace* in 2008), and eight volumes of published poetry (beginning with *Academic Notes* in 1974, and continuing up to *Late Harvest*, *Footprints*, and *Quiet Corners* in the years running up to 2008).

However, it is "Exploration and Exploitation in Organizational Learning" for which he is best known and that contains, in one work, the fruit of all his manifold theories and academic interests that he had previously spent much of an extremely fruitful and visible career, indeed both, exploring and exploiting.

While it is important to understand and be able to apply the most visible tools and concepts that people have taken from James March's "Exploration and Exploitation in Organizational Learning," it is equally important to understand the less well-known ones.

Combining insights from disciplines as broadly ranged as economics, psychology, and sociology, March invites readers to take a skeptical view of the organizations around them, to recognize that heterogeneity among an organization's members is vital for its ability to innovate, and that slow learners are as important as quick ones, not only in preserving its institutional memories, but also in exploring new discoveries.

With tools honed from "Exploration and Exploitation in Organizational Learning," a budding student of organizations is now in a position to begin doing this.

NOTES

1   "Workforce of the Future: The Competing Forces Shaping 2030," Price Waterhouse Cooper, August 15, 2017.

2   Richard M. Cyert and James G. March, *A Behavioral Theory of the Firm,* (1963), 2nd ed. (Oxford: Blackwell Publishers, 1992).

3   James G. March and Herbert A. Simon, *Organizations*, (New York: Wiley, 1958)

4   Mie Augier et al, "Perspective—The Flaring of Intellectual Outliers: An Organizational Interpretation of the Generation of Novelty in the RAND Corporation," *Organization Science* 26, no. 4, (2015): 1140-1161.

GLOSSARY

GLOSSARY OF TERMS

AirBnB: an American technology company founded in 2008, and which provides a marketplace for those wishing to lease or rent short-term lodging.

Behavioralism: an approach in political science that sought primarily to examine the actions of individuals rather than institutions, and first emerged in the 1930s, gaining ground between the 1940s and 1970s.

Behavioral Economics: a subfield of economics that studies the psychological and cognitive restraints on economic decisions by people and institutions. For behavioral economists, people are only rational to a limited degree (they refer to this as bounded rationality), by using shortcuts (also called heuristics), framing devices, and imperfect information. Actual decision-making, according to researchers in this subfield, therefore diverges from the pure rationality against a backdrop of perfect information predicted by neoclassical economists.

Bounded Rationality: the concept that individual decision making is constrained by the time available to make decisions, the extent of information which is on hand, and the limitations of the decision-maker's intellect.

Carnegie Institute of Technology (later Carnegie Mellon University): a private research university in Pittsburgh, Pennsylvania, founded in 1900. In 1967, the Carnegie Institute of Technology merged with the Mellon Institute of Industrial Research and became known as Carnegie Mellon University.

Carnegie School: a movement in economics based at the Carnegie Institute of Technology (after 1967, Carnegie Mellon University), and led by Herbert Simon, James March, and Richard Cyert. The school's predominant interest was in how organizations behave, a question to which its members applied insights from psychology, management studies, and decision analysis. A principal theme of the school's work was understanding why organizations might frequently behave in ways other than ones that are perfectly rational.

Collectivism: a cultural value which emphasizes cohesion within organizations and groups

Don Quixote: a Spanish novel published by Miguel de Cervantes in 1605 and 1615, and considered the most influential work of literature in the Spanish canon.

Entrepreneurialism: the activity of individuals who found and subsequently operate a corporate venture while assuming much of the risk involved.

Ethno-Political: relating to politics as it involves different ethnic groups, generally in competition.

Exploitation: In March's view, a business pursuing an advantage over competitors on the grounds of efficiency, execution, and refinement, rather than technological or product innovation.

Exploration: for March, this is a business's pursuit of new technologies and products to secure an advantage over competitors.

Freshwater Economists: researchers, especially in the early 1970s, who were located at universities along the North American Great Lakes, particularly the University of Chicago, Carnegie Mellon University, the University of Rochester, and Cornell University. As a research matter they tend to be interested in explaining how large ground behave in markets. As a matter of prescription, they tend to believe structural reform and low inflation should be predominant aims for government policy.

Garbage Can Model: an approach to understanding how organizations make decisions, first produced by James March and Johan Olsen in 1972. In this model, problems, solutions, and decision makers proceed in largely unrelated and disconnected paths, and are periodically mixed together in different ways like the contents of a garbage can.

Homogenous: a collection composed of things of the like kind.

McKinsey & Company: A worldwide management consultancy firm founded in 1926. It is the largest of the world's so-called "Big Three" largest consultancy firms, ahead of the Boston Consulting Group and Bain & Company.

Neoclassical Economics: a predominant approach within contemporary mainstream economics that rests on the assumptions that individuals have rational preferences about outcomes, people act independently on the basis of complete information, and firms maximize profits.

New Institutionalism: an approach which places emphasis on institutions in shaping the identities, preferences, and subsequently actions of people within them.

Organizational Theory: an approach within economics that studies organizations' decision processes and how these processes determine the organizations' performance. For March and scholars influenced by him, organizational theory constructs a political view of decision making in businesses, with the chief executive a political broker, and multiple other actors of different degrees of power.

Psychoanalysis: a discipline related to studying and treating the unconscious mind, established by Sigmund Freud in the early 1980s.

Rand McNally: a US publishing company that began in 1856 in Chicago, and gained prominence by producing railroad guides and atlases.

Seawater Economics: a term used to describe economists located in the coastal universities of the United States, especially in the early 1970s, who generally favored a larger role for government in moderating business cycles through public spending and adjustment of interest rates.

Silicon Valley: the southern portion of the area surrounding San Francisco Bay in the US state of California, so called from its large concentration of technology companies. The term gained widespread use in the early 1980s, when the area attracted a large number of semiconductor makers.

Stanford University: a private research university founded in 1891 and located in the US state of California, 20 miles from San Jose.

United Nations: an international organization established in 1945 and headquartered in New York City, with the aim of promoting international cooperation, peace, and security.

United States Military Academy: a federal service academy located in West Point, New York, 50 miles north of New York City, to train officers for the US army.

United States Naval Academy: a federal service academy established in 1845 and located in Annapolis, Maryland, to train officers for the US Navy and Marine Corps.

University of California, Irvine: a public research university created in 1965 and forming one of the ten campuses in the University of California system.

University of Wisconsin (or University of Wisconsin-Madison): a public research university in the state of Wisconsin that was founded in 1848.

War and Peace: a novel by Russian author Leo Tolstoy published in 1869, set in the Napoleonic wars and chronicling Napoleon's 1812 invasion of Russia.

Yale University: the third oldest institution of higher education in the US, founded in 1701 and located in New Haven, Connecticut. Yale is a private research university and forms part of the Ivy League.

PEOPLE MENTIONED IN THE TEXT

Michael Cohen (1945-2013) was a social scientist at the University of Michigan who held the position of William D. Hamilton Collegiate Professor of Complex Systems, Information, and Public Policy. In 1972, as a postdoctoral fellow at Stanford University, he worked with James March in formulating the Garbage Can model of organizational choice.

Richard Cyert (1921-1998) was an economist, organizational theorist, and statistician who served as president of Carnegie Mellon University. He was known for his work on the behavioral theory of the firm, which he coauthored with James March.

Angus Dawson is a senior partner in McKinsey & Company who leads the firm's strategy and corporate finance practice.

Sigmund Freud (1856-1939) was the founder of psychoanalysis, who qualified as a medical doctor at the University of Vienna and subsequently taught there as a professor.

Mikael Holmqvist (b. 1970) is a professor of business administration at Stockholm University, whose work concerns work, power, and organizations. He previously taught at Stanford and Cornell.

Richard Langlois (b. 1952) is a professor of economics at the University of Connecticut, who did his doctorate at Stanford while March was there. He is known for the Vanishing Hand theory, which said the visible hand of business managers slowly disappeared and was replaced by free market forces.

Charles Lindblom (b. 1917) is a political scientist and economist at Yale University, where he is Sterling Professor Emeritus of Political Science and Economics. He is a former president of the American Political Science Association, and known for his work on incrementalism, the view that most policy change is gradual and evolutionary rather than large and revolutionary.

Anne Miner is an emeritus professor at the University of Wisconsin-Madison's Wisconsin School of Business, whose research and teaching has focused on innovation, technology, and organizational learning.

Lawrence Mohr is an emeritus professor at the University of Michigan, whose main research area has been organization theory.

George Peter Murdock (1897-1985) was an anthropologist who was particularly known for constructing a large, empirical cross-cultural data set, which eventually grew to contain data for 1,200 cultures, coded in 100 variables. He also conducted research on family and kinship structures.

Johan Olsen (b. 1939) is a Norwegian political scientist and professor emeritus in political science at the University of Bergen. He helped to develop the Garbage Can model of how organizations make decisions.

John Padgett is a professor of political science at the University of Chicago, whose work has included a lengthy study modeling organizational innovation in Renaissance Florence.

Michael Polanyi (1891-1976) was a Hungarian-British academic who made seminal contributions to physical chemistry, economics, and philosophy. He was born in Budapest, worked in Germany, then accepted a chair at the University of Manchester, after which he became a senior research fellow at Merton College, Oxford.

Douglas Price was a lecturer in government at Columbia University, as well as a researcher in the Columbia Metropolitan Region Study Program.

Steven Shecter (b. 1956) is a documentary filmmaker from a Russian-American background who began his career by studying social anthropology at Harvard and working in the Smithsonian Institution's National Human Studies Film Center. An independent documentary producer since 1983, he worked on two films with James March.

Herbert Simon (1916–2001) was an American student of decision making who received the Turning Award in 1975 and the Novel Prize in Economics in 1978. He held the position of Richard King Mellon Professor at Carnegie Mellon University.

Charles Stauffacher (1920–2006) was executive vice president at the Continental Can Company, and later its vice chairman and chief financial officer. He also lectured in public administration at George Washington University.

Fred Strodtbeck (1919–2005) was a researcher in the way small groups interact, which he termed microsociology. He was professor of sociology and psychology at the University of Chicago, as well as a professor in its law school.

WORKS CITED

WORKS CITED

Adler, P., Goldoftas, B., & Levine, D. "Flexibility Versus Efficiency? A Case Study of Model Changeovers in The Toyota Production System." *Organization Science* 10 (1999):43-68.

Argyris, C., & Schön, D. *Organizational Learning: A Theory of Action Perspective.* Reading, Massachusetts: Addison-Wesley, 1978.

Augier, M. & March, J. "Realism and Comprehension in Economics: A Footnote to An Exchange Between Oliver E. Williamson And Herbert A. Simon." *Journal of Economic Behaviour and Organization* 66 (2008):97.

— "The Pursuit of Relevance in Management Education." *California Management Review* 49 (2007):129-146.

Badden-Fuller, C. & Volberda, H. "Strategic Renewal." *International Studies of Management and Organization* 27 (1997):95-120.

Bedeian, A. & Wren, D. "Most Influential Management Books of the 20th Century." *Organizational Dynamics* 29, no. 3 (2001): 221–225.

Benner, M. J., & Tushman, M. L. "Exploitation, Exploration, and Process Management: The Productivity Dilemma Revisited." *Academy of Management Review* 28 (2003): 238–256.

Burns, T. & Stalker, G. *The Management of Innovation.* London: Tavistock, 1961.

Collins, L. "Embedding Innovation into the Firm." *Research & Technology Management* 3, no. 4 (2007): 5-6.

Cyert, Richard M. & March, James G. *A Behavioral Theory of the Firm.* Englewood Cliffs, NJ: Prentice-Hall, 1963. 2nd ed., Oxford: Blackwell Publishers, 1992.

Duncan, R.B. "The Ambidextrous Organization: Designing Dual Structures for Innovation." In *The Management of Organization Design – Strategies And Implementation*, edited by R.H. Kilmann, L.R. Pondy and D.P. Slevin, 167-188. New York: Elsevier North-Holland, Inc., 1976.

Grant, R.M. "Prospering in Dynamically-Competitive Environments: Organizational Capability as Knowledge Integration." *Organization Science* 7, no. 4 (1996): 375-387.

Gupta, A., Smith, K. & Shalley, C. "The Interplay Between Exploration and Exploitation." *Academy of Management Journal* 49 (2006): 693-706.

He, Z. & Wong, P. "Exploration vs. Exploitation: An Empirical Test of The Ambidexterity Hypothesis." *Organizational Science* 15 (2004): 481-94.

Hindle, Tim. *Guide to Management Ideas and Gurus*. Suffolk: Profile Books Ltd, 2008.

Holland. J. *Adaptation in Natural and Artificial Systems: An Introduction Analysis with Application to Biology, Control And Artificial Intelligence*. Ann Arbor, MA: University of Michigan Press, 1975.

Katila, R. & Ahuja, G. "Something Old, Something New: A Longitudinal Study of Search Behavior and New Product Introduction." *Academy of Management Journal* 45 (2002):1183-94.

Laursen, K. & Salter, A. "Open for Innovation: The Role of Openness in Explaining Innovation Performance Among U.L. Manufacturing Firms." *Strategic Management Journal* 27 (2006):131-150.

Levinthal, D., & March, J. G. "The Myopia of Learning." *Strategic Management Journal* 14 (1993):95–112.

Levitt, B. & March, J. G. "Organizational learning." In W. R. Scott (Ed.), *Annual Review of Sociology* 14 (1988):319–340. Palo Alto, CA: Annual Reviews.

March, James G. *Decisions and Organizations.* New York: Basil Blackwell, 1988.

— "Rationality, Foolishness, and Adaptive Intelligence." *Strategic Management Journal* 27 (2006): 201-214.

— "Variable Risk Preferences and Adaptive Aspirations." *Journal of Economic Behavior and Organization* 9 (1988):5–24.

— "Continuity and Change in Theories of Organizational Action." *Administrative Science Quarterly* 41 (1996): 278-287.

— "Exploration and Exploitation in Organizational Learning." *Organizational Science* 2 (1991):71.

March, James G. & Olsen, Johan P. "Elaborating the 'New Institutionalism'." pp. 3-20 in R.A.W. Rhodes, S. Binder and B. Rockman (eds.) *The Oxford Handbook of Political Institutions*, Oxford: Oxford University Press, 2006.

— *Ambiguity and Choice in Organizations.* Bergen, Norway: Universitetsforlaget, 1976.

March, James G., Schulz, Martin & Zhou, Xueguang. *The Dynamics of Rules: Change in Written Organizational Codes*. Stanford, CA: Stanford University Press, 2000.

March, James G. and Simon, Herbert. "Organizations Revisited." *Industrial and Corporate Change* 2 (1993): 299-316.

— *Organizations.* New York: John Wiley & Sons, 1958.

March, James G. & Weil, Thierry. *On Leadership*. Oxford, UK: Blackwell Publishers, 2005.

Miller, K., Zhao, M. & Calantone, R. "Adding Interpersonal Learning and Tacit Knowledge to March's Exploration-Exploitation Model." *Academy of Management Journal* 49, no. 4, 2006: 709-722.

Mohr, L. "Ambiguity and Choice in Organizations (Review)." *American Political Science Review* 72, no. 3 (1978):1033-1035.

Oshri, I., Pan, S. & Newell, S. "Trade-Offs Between Knowledge Exploitation and Exploration Activities." *Knowledge Management Research & Practice* 3 (2005):10-23.

Puhan, Tatjana-Xenia. *Balancing Exploration and Exploitation by Creating Organizational Think Tanks*. Wiesbaden: Betriebswirtschaftlicher Verlag Dr. Th. Gabler / GWV Fachverlage GmbH, Wiesbaden, 2008.

Rao, H. & Drazin, R. "Overcoming resource constrains on product innovation by recruiting talent from rivals: a study of the mutual fund industry, 1986-94." *Academy of Management Journal* 45 (2002):491-507.

Rodan, S. "Exploration and Exploitation Revisited: Extending March's Model of Mutual Learning." *Scandinavian Journal of Management* 21, no. 4, (2005):407-428.

Rothaermel, F.T. "Incumbent's Advantage Through Exploiting Complementary Assets Via Interfirm Cooperation." *Strategic Management Journal* 22 (2001):687-699.

Tushman, M. & O'Reilly, C. "Ambidextrous Organizations: Managing Evolutionary and Revolutionary Change." *California Management Review* 38 (1996):8-30.

Vermeulen, F. & Barkema, H. "Learning Through Acquisitions." *Academy of Management Journal* 44 (2001):457-76.

Yelle, L. E. "The Learning Curve: Historical Review and Comprehensive Survey." *Decision Sciences* 10 (1979):302–328.

THE MACAT LIBRARY
BY DISCIPLINE

AFRICANA STUDIES

Chinua Achebe's *An Image of Africa: Racism in Conrad's Heart of Darkness*
W. E. B. Du Bois's *The Souls of Black Folk*
Zora Neale Huston's *Characteristics of Negro Expression*
Martin Luther King Jr's *Why We Can't Wait*
Toni Morrison's *Playing in the Dark: Whiteness in the American Literary Imagination*

ANTHROPOLOGY

Arjun Appadurai's *Modernity at Large: Cultural Dimensions of Globalisation*
Philippe Ariès's *Centuries of Childhood*
Franz Boas's *Race, Language and Culture*
Kim Chan & Renée Mauborgne's *Blue Ocean Strategy*
Jared Diamond's *Guns, Germs & Steel: the Fate of Human Societies*
Jared Diamond's *Collapse: How Societies Choose to Fail or Survive*
E. E. Evans-Pritchard's *Witchcraft, Oracles and Magic Among the Azande*
James Ferguson's *The Anti-Politics Machine*
Clifford Geertz's *The Interpretation of Cultures*
David Graeber's *Debt: the First 5000 Years*
Karen Ho's *Liquidated: An Ethnography of Wall Street*
Geert Hofstede's *Culture's Consequences: Comparing Values, Behaviors, Institutes and Organizations across Nations*
Claude Lévi-Strauss's *Structural Anthropology*
Jay Macleod's *Ain't No Makin' It: Aspirations and Attainment in a Low-Income Neighborhood*
Saba Mahmood's *The Politics of Piety: The Islamic Revival and the Feminist Subjec*t
Marcel Mauss's *The Gift*

BUSINESS

Jean Lave & Etienne Wenger's *Situated Learning*
Theodore Levitt's *Marketing Myopia*
Burton G. Malkiel's *A Random Walk Down Wall Street*
Douglas McGregor's *The Human Side of Enterprise*
Michael Porter's *Competitive Strategy: Creating and Sustaining Superior Performance*
John Kotter's *Leading Change*
C. K. Prahalad & Gary Hamel's *The Core Competence of the Corporation*

CRIMINOLOGY

Michelle Alexander's *The New Jim Crow: Mass Incarceration in the Age of Colorblindness*
Michael R. Gottfredson & Travis Hirschi's *A General Theory of Crime*
Richard Herrnstein & Charles A. Murray's *The Bell Curve: Intelligence and Class Structure in American Life*
Elizabeth Loftus's *Eyewitness Testimony*
Jay Macleod's *Ain't No Makin' It: Aspirations and Attainment in a Low-Income Neighborhood*
Philip Zimbardo's *The Lucifer Effect*

ECONOMICS

Janet Abu-Lughod's *Before European Hegemony*
Ha-Joon Chang's *Kicking Away the Ladder*
David Brion Davis's *The Problem of Slavery in the Age of Revolution*
Milton Friedman's *The Role of Monetary Policy*
Milton Friedman's *Capitalism and Freedom*
David Graeber's *Debt: the First 5000 Years*
Friedrich Hayek's *The Road to Serfdom*
Karen Ho's *Liquidated: An Ethnography of Wall Street*

The Macat Library By Discipline

John Maynard Keynes's *The General Theory of Employment, Interest and Money*
Charles P. Kindleberger's *Manias, Panics and Crashes*
Robert Lucas's *Why Doesn't Capital Flow from Rich to Poor Countries?*
Burton G. Malkiel's *A Random Walk Down Wall Street*
Thomas Robert Malthus's *An Essay on the Principle of Population*
Karl Marx's *Capital*
Thomas Piketty's *Capital in the Twenty-First Century*
Amartya Sen's *Development as Freedom*
Adam Smith's *The Wealth of Nations*
Nassim Nicholas Taleb's *The Black Swan: The Impact of the Highly Improbable*
Amos Tversky's & Daniel Kahneman's *Judgment under Uncertainty: Heuristics and Biases*
Mahbub Ul Haq's *Reflections on Human Development*
Max Weber's *The Protestant Ethic and the Spirit of Capitalism*

FEMINISM AND GENDER STUDIES

Judith Butler's *Gender Trouble*
Simone De Beauvoir's *The Second Sex*
Michel Foucault's *History of Sexuality*
Betty Friedan's *The Feminine Mystique*
Saba Mahmood's *The Politics of Piety: The Islamic Revival and the Feminist Subject*
Joan Wallach Scott's *Gender and the Politics of History*
Mary Wollstonecraft's *A Vindication of the Rights of Woman*
Virginia Woolf's *A Room of One's Own*

GEOGRAPHY

The Brundtland Report's *Our Common Future*
Rachel Carson's *Silent Spring*
Charles Darwin's *On the Origin of Species*
James Ferguson's *The Anti-Politics Machine*
Jane Jacobs's *The Death and Life of Great American Cities*
James Lovelock's *Gaia: A New Look at Life on Earth*
Amartya Sen's *Development as Freedom*
Mathis Wackernagel & William Rees's *Our Ecological Footprint*

HISTORY

Janet Abu-Lughod's *Before European Hegemony*
Benedict Anderson's *Imagined Communities*
Bernard Bailyn's *The Ideological Origins of the American Revolution*
Hanna Batatu's *The Old Social Classes And The Revolutionary Movements Of Iraq*
Christopher Browning's *Ordinary Men: Reserve Police Batallion 101 and the Final Solution in Poland*
Edmund Burke's *Reflections on the Revolution in France*
William Cronon's *Nature's Metropolis: Chicago And The Great West*
Alfred W. Crosby's *The Columbian Exchange*
Hamid Dabashi's *Iran: A People Interrupted*
David Brion Davis's *The Problem of Slavery in the Age of Revolution*
Nathalie Zemon Davis's *The Return of Martin Guerre*
Jared Diamond's *Guns, Germs & Steel: the Fate of Human Societies*
Frank Dikotter's *Mao's Great Famine*
John W Dower's *War Without Mercy: Race And Power In The Pacific War*
W. E. B. Du Bois's *The Souls of Black Folk*
Richard J. Evans's *In Defence of History*
Lucien Febvre's *The Problem of Unbelief in the 16th Century*
Sheila Fitzpatrick's *Everyday Stalinism*

Eric Foner's *Reconstruction: America's Unfinished Revolution, 1863-1877*
Michel Foucault's *Discipline and Punish*
Michel Foucault's *History of Sexuality*
Francis Fukuyama's *The End of History and the Last Man*
John Lewis Gaddis's *We Now Know: Rethinking Cold War History*
Ernest Gellner's *Nations and Nationalism*
Eugene Genovese's *Roll, Jordan, Roll: The World the Slaves Made*
Carlo Ginzburg's *The Night Battles*
Daniel Goldhagen's *Hitler's Willing Executioners*
Jack Goldstone's *Revolution and Rebellion in the Early Modern World*
Antonio Gramsci's *The Prison Notebooks*
Alexander Hamilton, John Jay & James Madison's *The Federalist Papers*
Christopher Hill's *The World Turned Upside Down*
Carole Hillenbrand's *The Crusades: Islamic Perspectives*
Thomas Hobbes's *Leviathan*
Eric Hobsbawm's *The Age Of Revolution*
John A. Hobson's *Imperialism: A Study*
Albert Hourani's *History of the Arab Peoples*
Samuel P. Huntington's *The Clash of Civilizations and the Remaking of World Order*
C. L. R. James's *The Black Jacobins*
Tony Judt's *Postwar: A History of Europe Since 1945*
Ernst Kantorowicz's *The King's Two Bodies: A Study in Medieval Political Theology*
Paul Kennedy's *The Rise and Fall of the Great Powers*
Ian Kershaw's *The "Hitler Myth": Image and Reality in the Third Reich*
John Maynard Keynes's *The General Theory of Employment, Interest and Money*
Charles P. Kindleberger's *Manias, Panics and Crashes*
Martin Luther King Jr's *Why We Can't Wait*
Henry Kissinger's *World Order: Reflections on the Character of Nations and the Course of History*
Thomas Kuhn's *The Structure of Scientific Revolutions*
Georges Lefebvre's *The Coming of the French Revolution*
John Locke's *Two Treatises of Government*
Niccolò Machiavelli's *The Prince*
Thomas Robert Malthus's *An Essay on the Principle of Population*
Mahmood Mamdani's *Citizen and Subject: Contemporary Africa And The Legacy Of Late Colonialism*
Karl Marx's *Capital*
Stanley Milgram's *Obedience to Authority*
John Stuart Mill's *On Liberty*
Thomas Paine's *Common Sense*
Thomas Paine's *Rights of Man*
Geoffrey Parker's *Global Crisis: War, Climate Change and Catastrophe in the Seventeenth Century*
Jonathan Riley-Smith's *The First Crusade and the Idea of Crusading*
Jean-Jacques Rousseau's *The Social Contract*
Joan Wallach Scott's *Gender and the Politics of History*
Theda Skocpol's *States and Social Revolutions*
Adam Smith's *The Wealth of Nations*
Timothy Snyder's *Bloodlands: Europe Between Hitler and Stalin*
Sun Tzu's *The Art of War*
Keith Thomas's *Religion and the Decline of Magic*
Thucydides's *The History of the Peloponnesian War*
Frederick Jackson Turner's *The Significance of the Frontier in American History*
Odd Arne Westad's *The Global Cold War: Third World Interventions And The Making Of Our Times*

LITERATURE

Chinua Achebe's *An Image of Africa: Racism in Conrad's Heart of Darkness*
Roland Barthes's *Mythologies*
Homi K. Bhabha's *The Location of Culture*
Judith Butler's *Gender Trouble*
Simone De Beauvoir's *The Second Sex*
Ferdinand De Saussure's *Course in General Linguistics*
T. S. Eliot's *The Sacred Wood: Essays on Poetry and Criticism*
Zora Neale Huston's *Characteristics of Negro Expression*
Toni Morrison's *Playing in the Dark: Whiteness in the American Literary Imagination*
Edward Said's *Orientalism*
Gayatri Chakravorty Spivak's *Can the Subaltern Speak?*
Mary Wollstonecraft's *A Vindication of the Rights of Women*
Virginia Woolf's *A Room of One's Own*

PHILOSOPHY

Elizabeth Anscombe's *Modern Moral Philosophy*
Hannah Arendt's *The Human Condition*
Aristotle's *Metaphysics*
Aristotle's *Nicomachean Ethics*
Edmund Gettier's *Is Justified True Belief Knowledge?*
Georg Wilhelm Friedrich Hegel's *Phenomenology of Spirit*
David Hume's *Dialogues Concerning Natural Religion*
David Hume's *The Enquiry for Human Understanding*
Immanuel Kant's *Religion within the Boundaries of Mere Reason*
Immanuel Kant's *Critique of Pure Reason*
Søren Kierkegaard's *The Sickness Unto Death*
Søren Kierkegaard's *Fear and Trembling*
C. S. Lewis's *The Abolition of Man*
Alasdair MacIntyre's *After Virtue*
Marcus Aurelius's *Meditations*
Friedrich Nietzsche's *On the Genealogy of Morality*
Friedrich Nietzsche's *Beyond Good and Evil*
Plato's *Republic*
Plato's *Symposium*
Jean-Jacques Rousseau's *The Social Contract*
Gilbert Ryle's *The Concept of Mind*
Baruch Spinoza's *Ethics*
Sun Tzu's *The Art of War*
Ludwig Wittgenstein's *Philosophical Investigations*

POLITICS

Benedict Anderson's *Imagined Communities*
Aristotle's *Politics*
Bernard Bailyn's *The Ideological Origins of the American Revolution*
Edmund Burke's *Reflections on the Revolution in France*
John C. Calhoun's *A Disquisition on Government*
Ha-Joon Chang's *Kicking Away the Ladder*
Hamid Dabashi's *Iran: A People Interrupted*
Hamid Dabashi's *Theology of Discontent: The Ideological Foundation of the Islamic Revolution in Iran*
Robert Dahl's *Democracy and its Critics*
Robert Dahl's *Who Governs?*
David Brion Davis's *The Problem of Slavery in the Age of Revolution*

Alexis De Tocqueville's *Democracy in America*
James Ferguson's *The Anti-Politics Machine*
Frank Dikotter's *Mao's Great Famine*
Sheila Fitzpatrick's *Everyday Stalinism*
Eric Foner's *Reconstruction: America's Unfinished Revolution, 1863-1877*
Milton Friedman's *Capitalism and Freedom*
Francis Fukuyama's *The End of History and the Last Man*
John Lewis Gaddis's *We Now Know: Rethinking Cold War History*
Ernest Gellner's *Nations and Nationalism*
David Graeber's *Debt: the First 5000 Years*
Antonio Gramsci's *The Prison Notebooks*
Alexander Hamilton, John Jay & James Madison's *The Federalist Papers*
Friedrich Hayek's *The Road to Serfdom*
Christopher Hill's *The World Turned Upside Down*
Thomas Hobbes's *Leviathan*
John A. Hobson's *Imperialism: A Study*
Samuel P. Huntington's *The Clash of Civilizations and the Remaking of World Order*
Tony Judt's *Postwar: A History of Europe Since 1945*
David C. Kang's *China Rising: Peace, Power and Order in East Asia*
Paul Kennedy's *The Rise and Fall of Great Powers*
Robert Keohane's *After Hegemony*
Martin Luther King Jr.'s *Why We Can't Wait*
Henry Kissinger's *World Order: Reflections on the Character of Nations and the Course of History*
John Locke's *Two Treatises of Government*
Niccolò Machiavelli's *The Prince*
Thomas Robert Malthus's *An Essay on the Principle of Population*
Mahmood Mamdani's *Citizen and Subject: Contemporary Africa And The Legacy Of
Late Colonialism*
Karl Marx's *Capital*
John Stuart Mill's *On Liberty*
John Stuart Mill's *Utilitarianism*
Hans Morgenthau's *Politics Among Nations*
Thomas Paine's *Common Sense*
Thomas Paine's *Rights of Man*
Thomas Piketty's *Capital in the Twenty-First Century*
Robert D. Putman's *Bowling Alone*
John Rawls's *Theory of Justice*
Jean-Jacques Rousseau's *The Social Contract*
Theda Skocpol's *States and Social Revolutions*
Adam Smith's *The Wealth of Nations*
Sun Tzu's *The Art of War*
Henry David Thoreau's *Civil Disobedience*
Thucydides's *The History of the Peloponnesian War*
Kenneth Waltz's *Theory of International Politics*
Max Weber's *Politics as a Vocation*
Odd Arne Westad's *The Global Cold War: Third World Interventions And The Making Of Our Times*

POSTCOLONIAL STUDIES

Roland Barthes's *Mythologies*
Frantz Fanon's *Black Skin, White Masks*
Homi K. Bhabha's *The Location of Culture*
Gustavo Gutiérrez's *A Theology of Liberation*
Edward Said's *Orientalism*
Gayatri Chakravorty Spivak's *Can the Subaltern Speak?*

PSYCHOLOGY

Gordon Allport's *The Nature of Prejudice*
Alan Baddeley & Graham Hitch's *Aggression: A Social Learning Analysis*
Albert Bandura's *Aggression: A Social Learning Analysis*
Leon Festinger's *A Theory of Cognitive Dissonance*
Sigmund Freud's *The Interpretation of Dreams*
Betty Friedan's *The Feminine Mystique*
Michael R. Gottfredson & Travis Hirschi's *A General Theory of Crime*
Eric Hoffer's *The True Believer: Thoughts on the Nature of Mass Movements*
William James's *Principles of Psychology*
Elizabeth Loftus's *Eyewitness Testimony*
A. H. Maslow's *A Theory of Human Motivation*
Stanley Milgram's *Obedience to Authority*
Steven Pinker's *The Better Angels of Our Nature*
Oliver Sacks's *The Man Who Mistook His Wife For a Hat*
Richard Thaler & Cass Sunstein's *Nudge: Improving Decisions About Health, Wealth and Happiness*
Amos Tversky's *Judgment under Uncertainty: Heuristics and Biases*
Philip Zimbardo's *The Lucifer Effect*

SCIENCE

Rachel Carson's *Silent Spring*
William Cronon's *Nature's Metropolis: Chicago And The Great West*
Alfred W. Crosby's *The Columbian Exchange*
Charles Darwin's *On the Origin of Species*
Richard Dawkin's *The Selfish Gene*
Thomas Kuhn's *The Structure of Scientific Revolutions*
Geoffrey Parker's *Global Crisis: War, Climate Change and Catastrophe in the Seventeenth Century*
Mathis Wackernagel & William Rees's *Our Ecological Footprint*

SOCIOLOGY

Michelle Alexander's *The New Jim Crow: Mass Incarceration in the Age of Colorblindness*
Gordon Allport's *The Nature of Prejudice*
Albert Bandura's *Aggression: A Social Learning Analysis*
Hanna Batatu's *The Old Social Classes And The Revolutionary Movements Of Iraq*
Ha-Joon Chang's *Kicking Away the Ladder*
W. E. B. Du Bois's *The Souls of Black Folk*
Émile Durkheim's *On Suicide*
Frantz Fanon's *Black Skin, White Masks*
Frantz Fanon's *The Wretched of the Earth*
Eric Foner's *Reconstruction: America's Unfinished Revolution, 1863-1877*
Eugene Genovese's *Roll, Jordan, Roll: The World the Slaves Made*
Jack Goldstone's *Revolution and Rebellion in the Early Modern World*
Antonio Gramsci's *The Prison Notebooks*
Richard Herrnstein & Charles A Murray's *The Bell Curve: Intelligence and Class Structure in American Life*
Eric Hoffer's *The True Believer: Thoughts on the Nature of Mass Movements*
Jane Jacobs's *The Death and Life of Great American Cities*
Robert Lucas's *Why Doesn't Capital Flow from Rich to Poor Countries?*
Jay Macleod's *Ain't No Makin' It: Aspirations and Attainment in a Low Income Neighborhood*
Elaine May's *Homeward Bound: American Families in the Cold War Era*
Douglas McGregor's *The Human Side of Enterprise*
C. Wright Mills's *The Sociological Imagination*

Thomas Piketty's *Capital in the Twenty-First Century*
Robert D. Putman's *Bowling Alone*
David Riesman's *The Lonely Crowd: A Study of the Changing American Character*
Edward Said's *Orientalism*
Joan Wallach Scott's *Gender and the Politics of History*
Theda Skocpol's *States and Social Revolutions*
Max Weber's *The Protestant Ethic and the Spirit of Capitalism*

THEOLOGY

Augustine's *Confessions*
Benedict's *Rule of St Benedict*
Gustavo Gutiérrez's *A Theology of Liberation*
Carole Hillenbrand's *The Crusades: Islamic Perspectives*
David Hume's *Dialogues Concerning Natural Religion*
Immanuel Kant's *Religion within the Boundaries of Mere Reason*
Ernst Kantorowicz's *The King's Two Bodies: A Study in Medieval Political Theology*
Søren Kierkegaard's *The Sickness Unto Death*
C. S. Lewis's *The Abolition of Man*
Saba Mahmood's *The Politics of Piety: The Islamic Revival and the Feminist Subject*
Baruch Spinoza's *Ethics*
Keith Thomas's *Religion and the Decline of Magic*

COMING SOON

Chris Argyris's *The Individual and the Organisation*
Seyla Benhabib's *The Rights of Others*
Walter Benjamin's *The Work Of Art in the Age of Mechanical Reproduction*
John Berger's *Ways of Seeing*
Pierre Bourdieu's *Outline of a Theory of Practice*
Mary Douglas's *Purity and Danger*
Roland Dworkin's *Taking Rights Seriously*
James G. March's *Exploration and Exploitation in Organisational Learning*
Ikujiro Nonaka's *A Dynamic Theory of Organizational Knowledge Creation*
Griselda Pollock's *Vision and Difference*
Amartya Sen's *Inequality Re-Examined*
Susan Sontag's *On Photography*
Yasser Tabbaa's *The Transformation of Islamic Art*
Ludwig von Mises's *Theory of Money and Credit*

Macat Disciplines

Access the greatest ideas and thinkers across entire disciplines, including

Postcolonial Studies

Roland Barthes's *Mythologies*
Frantz Fanon's *Black Skin, White Masks*
Homi K. Bhabha's *The Location of Culture*
Gustavo Gutiérrez's *A Theology of Liberation*
Edward Said's *Orientalism*
Gayatri Chakravorty Spivak's *Can the Subaltern Speak?*

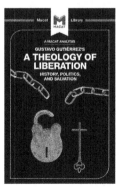
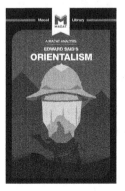

Macat analyses are available from all good bookshops and libraries.

Access hundreds of analyses through one, multimedia tool.
Join free for one month **library.macat.com**

Macat Disciplines

Access the greatest ideas and thinkers across entire disciplines, including

AFRICANA STUDIES

Chinua Achebe's *An Image of Africa:
Racism in Conrad's Heart of Darkness*

W. E. B. Du Bois's *The Souls of Black Folk*

Zora Neale Hurston's *Characteristics of Negro Expression*

Martin Luther King Jr.'s *Why We Can't Wait*

Toni Morrison's *Playing in the Dark:
Whiteness in the American Literary Imagination*

Macat analyses are available from all good bookshops and libraries.

Access hundreds of analyses through one, multimedia tool.
Join free for one month **library.macat.com**

Macat Disciplines

Access the greatest ideas and thinkers across entire disciplines, including

FEMINISM, GENDER AND QUEER STUDIES

Simone De Beauvoir's
The Second Sex

Michel Foucault's
History of Sexuality

Betty Friedan's
The Feminine Mystique

Saba Mahmood's
*The Politics of Piety:
The Islamic Revival and
the Feminist Subject*

Joan Wallach Scott's
*Gender and the
Politics of History*

Mary Wollstonecraft's
*A Vindication of the
Rights of Woman*

Virginia Woolf's
A Room of One's Own

Judith Butler's
Gender Trouble

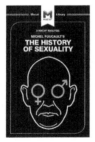

Macat analyses are available from all good bookshops and libraries.

Access hundreds of analyses through one, multimedia tool.
Join free for one month **library.macat.com**

Macat Disciplines

Access the greatest ideas and thinkers across entire disciplines, including

CRIMINOLOGY

Michelle Alexander's
*The New Jim Crow:
Mass Incarceration in the
Age of Colorblindness*

**Michael R. Gottfredson
& Travis Hirschi's**
A General Theory of Crime

Elizabeth Loftus's
Eyewitness Testimony

**Richard Herrnstein
& Charles A. Murray's**
*The Bell Curve: Intelligence and
Class Structure in American Life*

Jay Macleod's
*Ain't No Makin' It:
Aspirations and Attainment in a
Low-Income Neighborhood*

Philip Zimbardo's
The Lucifer Effect

Macat Disciplines

Access the greatest ideas and thinkers across entire disciplines, including

INEQUALITY

Ha-Joon Chang's, *Kicking Away the Ladder*

David Graeber's, *Debt: The First 5000 Years*

Robert E. Lucas's, *Why Doesn't Capital Flow from Rich To Poor Countries?*

Thomas Piketty's, *Capital in the Twenty-First Century*

Amartya Sen's, *Inequality Re-Examined*

Mahbub Ul Haq's, *Reflections on Human Development*

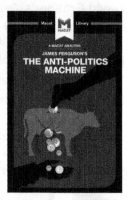

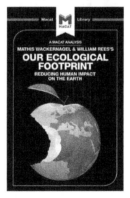

Macat Disciplines

Access the greatest ideas and thinkers across entire disciplines, including

THE FUTURE OF DEMOCRACY

Robert A. Dahl's, *Democracy and Its Critics*
Robert A. Dahl's, *Who Governs?*
Alexis De Toqueville's, *Democracy in America*
Niccolò Machiavelli's, *The Prince*
John Stuart Mill's, *On Liberty*
Robert D. Putnam's, *Bowling Alone*
Jean-Jacques Rousseau's, *The Social Contract*
Henry David Thoreau's, *Civil Disobedience*

Macat Disciplines

Access the greatest ideas and thinkers across entire disciplines, including

TOTALITARIANISM

Sheila Fitzpatrick's, *Everyday Stalinism*
Ian Kershaw's, *The "Hitler Myth"*
Timothy Snyder's, *Bloodlands*

Macat Pairs

Analyse historical and modern issues from opposite sides of an argument. Pairs include:

RACE AND IDENTITY

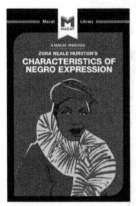

Zora Neale Hurston's
Characteristics of Negro Expression

Using material collected on anthropological expeditions to the South, Zora Neale Hurston explains how expression in African American culture in the early twentieth century departs from the art of white America. At the time, African American art was often criticized for copying white culture. For Hurston, this criticism misunderstood how art works. European tradition views art as something fixed. But Hurston describes a creative process that is alive, ever-changing, and largely improvisational. She maintains that African American art works through a process called 'mimicry'—where an imitated object or verbal pattern, for example, is reshaped and altered until it becomes something new, novel—and worthy of attention.

Frantz Fanon's
Black Skin, White Masks

Black Skin, White Masks offers a radical analysis of the psychological effects of colonization on the colonized.

Fanon witnessed the effects of colonization first hand both in his birthplace, Martinique, and again later in life when he worked as a psychiatrist in another French colony, Algeria. His text is uncompromising in form and argument. He dissects the dehumanizing effects of colonialism, arguing that it destroys the native sense of identity, forcing people to adapt to an alien set of values—including a core belief that they are inferior. This results in deep psychological trauma.

Fanon's work played a pivotal role in the civil rights movements of the 1960s.

Macat analyses are available from all good bookshops and libraries.

Access hundreds of analyses through one, multimedia tool.
Join free for one month **library.macat.com**